L4057/22

D0682244

PRACTITIONER RESEARCH
IN EARLY CHILDHOOD

⊕SAGE | 50 YEARS

SAGE was founded in 1965 by Sara Miller McCune to support
the dissemination of usable knowledge by publishing innovative
and high-quality research and teaching content. Today, we
publish more than 850 journals, including those of more than
300 learned societies, more than 800 new books per year, and
a growing range of library products including archives, data,
case studies, reports, and video. SAGE remains majority-owned
by our founder, and after Sara's lifetime will become owned by
a charitable trust that secures our continued independence.

Los Angeles | London | New Delhi | Singapore | Washington DC

PRACTITIONER RESEARCH
IN EARLY CHILDHOOD

International Issues and Perspectives

Edited by
LINDA NEWMAN & CHRISTINE WOODROW

LRC Stoke Park
GUILDFORD COLLEGE

Los Angeles | London | New Delhi
Singapore | Washington DC

188990   372.
21072
NEW

RESEARCH
SKILLS

Los Angeles | London | New Delhi
Singapore | Washington DC

SAGE Publications Ltd
1 Oliver's Yard
55 City Road
London EC1Y 1SP

SAGE Publications Inc.
2455 Teller Road
Thousand Oaks, California 91320

SAGE Publications India Pvt Ltd
B 1/I 1 Mohan Cooperative Industrial Area
Mathura Road
New Delhi 110 044

SAGE Publications Asia-Pacific Pte Ltd
3 Church Street
#10-04 Samsung Hub
Singapore 049483

Editor: Jude Bowen
Assistant editor: George Knowles
Production editor: Nicola Marshall
Copyeditor: Gemma Marren
Proofreader: Emily Ayers
Marketing executive: Dilhara Attygalle
Cover design: Wendy Scott
Typeset by: C&M Digitals (P) Ltd, Chennai, India

Editorial Arrangement © Linda Newman and Christine
Woodrow 2015, Chapter 1 © Christine Woodrow and Linda
Newman 2015, Chapter 2 © Linda Newman, Christine
Woodrow, Silvia Rójo and Mónica Galvez 2015, Chapter 3 ©
Oznur Aydemir, Fatima Mourad, Leonie Arthur and Jen
Skattebol 2015, Chapter 4 © Lyn Fasoli and Alison
Wunungmurra 2015, Chapter 5 © Karin Rönnerman 2015,
Chapter 6 © Norma Rudolph and Mary James 2015,
Chapter 7 © Linda Newman, Janet Keegan and Trish Heeley
2015, Chapter 8 © Nicole Mockler and Ashley Casey 2015

First published 2015.

Apart from any fair dealing for the purposes of research or
private study, or criticism or review, as permitted under the
Copyright, Designs and Patents Act, 1988, this publication
may be reproduced, stored or transmitted in any form, or by
any means, only with the prior permission in writing of the
publishers, or in the case of reprographic reproduction, in
accordance with the terms of licences issued by the
Copyright Licensing Agency. Enquiries concerning
reproduction outside those terms should be sent to the
publishers.

Library of Congress Control Number: 2014959830

British Library Cataloguing in Publication data

A catalogue record for this book is available from
the British Library

ISBN 978-1-4462-9534-2
ISBN 978-1-4462-9535-9 (pbk)

At SAGE we take sustainability seriously. Most of our products are printed in the UK using FSC papers and boards.
When we print overseas we ensure sustainable papers are used as measured by the Egmont grading system.
We undertake an annual audit to monitor our sustainability.

CONTENTS

WITHDRAWN

ABOUT THE EDITORS

Linda Newman (EdD; MEd Hons; BEd (EC); Dip Teach (EC)) is the Chair of Early Childhood and Primary Programs in the School of Education at The University of Newcastle, Australia and Chair of the Early Childhood Teacher Education Council (NSW). She is a team member of Futuro Infantil Hoy (FIH), an ongoing international research and development project in Chile. Linda's research aims to theorise and apply ethical approaches that facilitate equity and benefit. Influential conceptual framings include socio-cultural theory, new sociologies of childhood; community and family capacity building; valuing of diversity and 'funds of knowledge'; play-based intentional teaching and sustained shared thinking; and literacy as social practice. Website: www.newcastle.edu.au/staff/research-profile/Linda_Newman/

Christine Woodrow (PhD; MEd; BEd, DipT ECE) is deputy director of the Centre for Educational Research at the University of Western Sydney and is project leader of Futuro Infantil Hoy, an ongoing international research and development project in early childhood education being undertaken within a unique strategic alliance involving Fundación Minera Escondida, the University of Western Sydney and early childhood service providers in Chile. She is a member of the Globalisation research group, where her research is focused on international policy and practice in early childhood education, educational leadership and the professional preparation of early childhood educators. Website: www.uws.edu.au/cer

ABOUT THE CONTRIBUTORS

Leonie Arthur is a senior lecturer in early childhood education at the University of Western Sydney, Australia. She is a team member of Futuro Infantil Hoy, a community capacity building research project in Chile. She is interested in teachers' pedagogies and teacher identities and the role of practitioner research in building contextually responsive curriculum that engages children in learning. She has been involved with a number of practitioner research projects aimed at generating new knowledge in early childhood education and care.

Oznur Aydemir is a graduate of early childhood education from the University of Western Sydney, Australia and has been working in Islamic schools in Sydney, Australia for seven years, predominantly teaching in the early years of school and coordinating and teaching drama work-shops for students. Her interest lies in demystifying the stereotyping of Muslims as carrying exclusive forms of being, often embedded in Orientalist discourses. She is also interested in exploring the inclusion of spirituality in teacher education programmes and the workings of spiritu-ality in schools by students and teachers. Oznur took part in practitioner research because it offered a trusting space for Muslim practitioners to share, discuss and bring together a research study without feeling the shadow of scrutiny and criticism often seen in the media, and at times experienced in public spaces in Sydney.

Ashley Casey is a lecturer in pedagogy in the School of Sport, Exercise and Health Sciences at Loughborough University, UK. He started his career as a secondary school physical education teacher, a position he held for 15 years, and it was in this role, as a full-time teacher, that he engaged in practitioner research over the seven years of his part-time Masters and PhD. He has published in the *Educational Action Research Journal* about his experiences as a practitioner researcher and currently supports teacher learning, reflection and use of research through his weekly blog (www.peprn.com) and podcast 'major themes in physical education research'. He is currently working on a practitioner research book for physical education and youth sport professionals and is an active member of the physical education community on Twitter. In addition to this work he is an adjunct senior lecturer in the Department of Physical Education and Sport Sciences at the University of Limerick, Ireland and co-convenor of the Physical Education and Sport Pedagogy special interest group in the British Educational Research Association.

Lyn Fasoli has worked in the field of early childhood for many years, beginning as a teacher of young children in centre-based childcare, out of school hours care, preschool and school classrooms and in a mobile children's service. She is an American-Australian who has lived in Australia since 1972 and is Associate Professor in the Higher Education and Research Division at Batchelor Institute of Indigenous Tertiary Education where her research focuses on indigenous education, early childhood education and care, children's services training and development and leadership practices. She is the mother of one son and has four grandsons. She completed her Doctorate at the University of Canberra in 2003 where her research investigated preschool aged children's learning in the museum and art gallery as entry into new 'communities of practice'.

Mónica Galvez is a Chilean educator leader and director in the Fundación Minera Escondida early childhood centre, that operates under the auspices of JUNJI (the national Chilean early childhood organisation), and is a host institution for the pilot of the Futuro Infantil Hoy project. She has worked at the centre for 20 years and led the centre through its three year participation in FIH and has established the centre as a point of reference for excellence and quality early childhood education in the region.

Trish Heeley is an early childhood educator with 25 years' experience working as a practitioner within the early childhood profession in a variety of roles and an early childhood student currently working towards her Master of Education with Honours through the University of New England, Australia. She is currently the (Australian) National Quality Framework

Implementation Coordinator for Penrith City Council and in this role provides support to a large number of services in delivering quality programmes to children in the Local Government Area. She was a founding member of the council's Curriculum Renewal Project aimed at providing ongoing training to all council educators in relation to contemporary reflexive practice. Trish has a deep interest in the way curriculum supports the delivery of quality services to young children and their families and her involvement in practitioner research was inspired by this interest.

Mary James is the director of Little Elephant Training Centre for Early Education (LETCEE), Greytown, South Africa. Little Elephant is a non-profit early childhood development (ECD) resource and training organisation in Kwa Zulu Natal, South Africa. Mary's primary concern is for the young children who are especially vulnerable as a result of poverty and social inequality, and the focus of her work is on strengthening the capacity of practitioners and parents to create nurturing communities for children. She was awarded an honorary doctorate by Anglia Ruskin University, Chelmsford, UK in recognition of her pioneering work in family-based ECD programmes in the region.

Janet Keegan is the manager of Children's Services for Penrith City Council in New South Wales, Australia. Janet has worked as a practitioner in the early/middle childhood field for many years, much of this time spent coordinating an outreach mobile service for isolated families. Janet has also spent some time as an adult trainer. She has a keen interest in researching children's play and intentional teaching and was a founding member of the council's Children's Services Curriculum Renewal Group (CRG), the main focus of which is providing professional development to centre educators relating to contemporary reflexive practice.

Nicole Mockler was a senior lecturer in the School of Education at The University of Newcastle, Australia at the time of writing. She has since moved to the University of Sydney. Her background is as a secondary school teacher, school leader and professional development consultant. Nicole's research interests include teacher professional learning and identity and the politics of education, and she has a particular interest in exploring the links between education policy and teachers' professional practice. Her recent books include *Big Fish, Little Fish: Teaching and Learning in the Middle Years* (with Susan Groundwater-Smith, Cambridge University Press, 2015), *Engaging in Student Voice in Research, Education and Community: Beyond Legitimation and Guardianship* (with Susan Groundwater-Smith, Springer, 2014) and *Facilitating Practitioner Research: Developing Transformational*

Partnerships (with Susan Groundwater-Smith, Jane Mitchell, Petra Ponte and Karin Rönnerman, Routledge, 2013).

Fatima Mourad is an early childhood teacher education graduate currently working as a director of an early childhood centre in Liverpool, Sydney, Australia. She is interested in practitioner research because of the leadership qualities and skills it provides to practitioners in the early childhood field. As a Muslim, she believes it provides an opportunity for Muslim voices to be heard and responded to within the educational field and at the same time provides opportunities to integrate Islamic knowledge into the field of education.

Silvia Rójo is an early childhood educator in Chile, formerly an early childhood centre director and now playing a key role as senior mentor to early childhood centres implementing the Futuro Infantil Hoy project in Northern Chile. She led her own centre through their participation in the pilot of FIH and has been passionately interested in how practitioner research mobilises change. Silvia studied three years of Pedagogy in Educational Technology and then changed to Early Childhood Education. She has worked as a teacher in centres and schools, as a computer teacher and as a school counsellor. Since joining the FIH project Silvia has lectured at university, worked in an educational computer-based project, commenced Masters study in educational management and is studying a Diploma in Quality Management.

Karin Rönnerman is a professor in education at the Department of Education and Special Education, University of Gothenburg, Sweden. She is the leader of a Masters programme in education and action research. In 2004, she received a joint commission from the Swedish National Agency for School Improvement and one of the national teaching unions to develop a course in action research focusing on quality in preschools. She has followed some of the early childhood teachers participating in the course and has facilitated them to become leaders of practitioner research in their own schools. She also teaches at PhD level and supervises five doctoral candidates, all researching versions of action research. Her main research interests are action research, professional development, professional learning communities and partnerships between university and school.

Norma Rudolph has four decades of experience in education and development in a wide range of contexts, both rural and urban, with government and non-government organisations. She has extensive experience in policy development and the design, delivery and evaluation of programmes within the context of early childhood development, primary and secondary schooling, adult education, community development and professional development for teachers. Her research interests include action research, policy and evaluation with a special focus on social justice and appreciative inquiry. As senior researcher in the Children's Institute at the University of Cape Town in South Africa she led the Caring Schools Action Research Project. She also led a trans-disciplinary review of education, health and social service policies in the 16 countries making up the Southern African Development Community (SADC) and developed a framework for mainstreaming care and support in the education sector for implementation across the whole SADC region. She is currently a PhD candidate at The University of Newcastle, Australia.

Jen Skattebol works at the Social Policy Research Centre at the University of New South Wales, Australia. Jen has worked in early childhood settings and in teacher education. Her research primarily focuses on social inclusion. Her doctoral work made theoretical contributions to the sociology of childhood and theorised the transformative potential of practitioner inquiry and on the recommendations of her examiners has been subsequently published as *(Re)searching for shared meanings between teachers and children: identities – being and belonging* (2010, Saarbrueken: VDM Verlag). Between 2007 and 2009 she was involved in a series of practitioner research projects aimed at generating new knowledge in early childhood education and care. Currently, she is investigating low-income families' experiences of the early childhood education and care sector.

Alison Wunungmurra is a Dhalangu woman from North East Arnhemland in the Northern Territory of Australia. She grew up in a small island community called Milingimbi and lived at another remote community, Gapuwiyak, until January 2008. She has been a worker and the director at her local childcare centre and a council member in her community. She has worked as a childcare trainer and early childhood researcher at the Batchelor Institute of Indigenous Tertiary Education and is completing the final year of her BEd in early childhood. She is the mother of seven children and has one grandchild.

PREFACE

The idea for this book arose from our ongoing experiences as academic partners in a range of practitioner research initiatives in diverse early childhood contexts in Australia and Chile. These experiences have provided us with a growing conviction that the practitioner research paradigm is characterised by a powerful set of methodologies for growing pedagogical leadership and supporting sustainable change and that its potential is under-appreciated, undervalued and underutilised, especially in early childhood situations. Our objectives in bringing together a range of research stories – told from different perspectives in contexts as diverse as South Africa, Chile, Australia and Sweden – are to demonstrate the methodologies in action, raise significant and sometimes contested issues related to their implementation – for example, issues of voice and power, the nature of partnership – and to resource and inspire practitioners, service providers, policy-makers, funders and academics to incorporate these approaches in their repertoire of resources for supporting leadership development, strengthening pedagogical practices and promoting the quality of early childhood practice.

We would like to acknowledge our employing institutions, the Faculty of Education and Arts at The University of Newcastle and the Centre for Educational Research at the University of Western Sydney for supporting our work in producing this volume. It would not have been possible without the many practitioners that we have had the privilege of working with over many years. We also appreciate and thank our co-contributors for the intellectual rigour of their chapters, their generosity and good humour. The writing process has not always been straightforward. Mirroring life, during the course of the book's development, members of the writing team faced personal loss, health challenges and personal crises themselves or within their families. Nevertheless their commitment and our determination to share these uplifting stories carried us through.

We hope the readers find reading the research stories as rewarding and inspiring as we have found assembling them.

Linda Newman and Christine Woodrow

ACKNOWLEDGEMENTS

The authors of Chapter 2 acknowledge the educators, families and children who participated in the Futuro Infantil Hoy research project and the support of the Fundación Minera Escondida, Chile, which funded the project 2008–2014.

The authors of Chapter 4 wish to acknowledge the research participants from the community of Gapuwiyak, the Telstra Foundation, co-researchers Jude Maglis, Anna Godden, Veronica Pompei and Ranu James, evaluator Kaye Lowe and reference group members Veronica Johns, Karen Martin and Barbara Piscitelli, all of whom contributed to their thinking, but the views expressed in the chapter are their own.

The authors of Chapter 7 wish to thank the Jean Denton Scholarship held by Linda Newman for the opportunity to commence the work described in this chapter. They also wish to thank Ms Denise Gibson and Ms Anne Cipants for their formative conversations that helped spark the plan for the Jean Denton Project and Ms Kim Nasner who worked to develop the CRG before she moved to another region.

1

RECOGNISING, VALUING AND CELEBRATING PRACTITIONER RESEARCH

Christine Woodrow and Linda Newman

Practitioner research has become a recognised and legitimate form of professional learning in many professional contexts, and a significant component of what has been identified as a 'paradigm shift gathering momentum' in relation to the professional learning of teachers that goes beyond 'merely supporting the acquisition of new knowledge and skills' (Vescio et al., 2008: 81). An established research literature demonstrates the contribution its use makes to sustaining educational change, quality improvement and teacher growth and empowerment in school settings (see, for example, Cochran-Smith and Lytle, 2007; Groundwater-Smith and Mockler, 2008; Kemmis et al., 2014; Mockler and Casey, this volume). In contrast, in early childhood contexts, practitioner research might be seen as an 'emergent' practice, and the research literature documenting its use in these settings, while growing, is relatively small. This is both perplexing, given the growth in policy attention internationally to early childhood, and the consequent need to strengthen pedagogical quality and 'grow' the profession, and unsurprising, given the often marginal status of the early childhood profession and the increasingly dominant framing of early childhood within human capital discourses (Bown et al., 2009; Moss, 2012). In this chapter, we establish the rationale for the production of this book and its contribution to understanding and exemplifying the important place of practitioner research in the early childhood field. The chapter begins with a brief overview of the research and policy context of early childhood. This is followed by an articulation of what is understood and implied by practitioner research and its variant forms, incorporating a discussion of its distinctive characteristics and contribution. The final section of this chapter introduces the chapters of the book and discusses their content and contribution under the particular themes of collaborative partnerships, knowledge and knowing, capacity building and transformation and change. These themes were identified by the editors as particularly salient from the research findings of projects described by the chapter authors.

The early childhood policy and research context

Although internationally early childhood is a field of practice with a long and often vibrant history, in many countries its place has only recently moved from existing 'on the margins' to the mainstream of education/ social policy and its practitioners accorded recognition of their professional status, as reflected in their professional identity, learning opportunities and pay and conditions. In other places, particularly in majority nations, this recognition is yet to occur, so in many contexts, the recognition of professional status is at best ambiguous. Further, the theoretical framings of early childhood education have historically been rooted in discourses of child development, stage theory and scientific research models, reinforcing notions of knowledge as fixed and universal, and research as something undertaken by more knowing 'others'. Such conceptualisations offer little space and few resources for thinking about practitioner agency and knowledge as contestable and locally situated. Accompanying the increasing prominence of early childhood in government agendas, and the consequent expansion in early childhood services, there has also been a strengthening conceptualisation of early childhood that invokes human capital and regulatory discourses within neoliberal frameworks of accountability, the effects of which are eloquently explained by Moss (2007) and others. These discourses have resulted in increasing codification of practice (Sumsion et al., 2009; Woodrow and Brennan, 1999), proliferating regulatory requirements and increased accountability through standards and competency frameworks (Miller, 2008; Osgood, 2006), resulting in practitioners experiencing what has been described as a 'regulatory burden' (Fenech et al., 2006, 2008; Fenech and Sumsion, 2007a, 2007b). According to some early childhood researchers, these

developments threaten the empowerment of early childhood practitioners, their professional autonomy and suppression of their leadership
aspirations (Skattebol and Arthur, 2014), and are reductionist by promoting an understanding of professional practice as the demonstration of
technical competence (Osgood, 2006).

These conditions work to 'technologies' early childhood professional
practice (Dahlberg et al., 2007), and result in the prescription of norms to
which practitioners must conform. Osgood (2006, 2010) argues that this
puts at risk alternative constructions of early childhood professionalism
that acknowledge the relationality and complexity of early childhood
work, and in which critical reflection and the practice of autonomous
professional decision-making are features. Such divergent constructions
of the early childhood pedagogical space have implications for the kind
of professional learning made available to the profession. Technicist constructions favour professional learning models in which knowledge is
perceived as fixed and universal, fostering skill development and compliance, and these reflect the dominant discourse. Alternative models in
which early childhood educators are constructed as site-based researchers
involved in the production of localised, contextually relevant knowledge
experience greater difficulty in gaining traction, and hence attracting
funding support and institutional commitment; an aspect of which the
authors have considerable experience.

However, practitioner research might be seen as an ideal methodology that responds to the pressures of these contextual features and might
usefully contribute to the need to build a more nuanced repertoire of
pedagogical practice (Mitchell and Cubey, 2003), the creation of conceptual resources for building local community and pedagogical adaptive
leadership capacity (Skattebol and Arthur, 2014; Woodrow, 2011), a
better understanding and recognition of the relational and emotional
dimensions of early childhood work (Taggart, 2011), practitioners' will-
ingness to research their own practice (Newman and Mowbray, 2012),
and harnessing the well documented 'passion' that characterises practitioners' engagement in the field (Moyles, 2001; Osgood, 2010; Pardo
and Woodrow, 2014). At the same time, there is what might be characterised as a current flourishing of research in the early childhood field,
particularly within post-colonial, post-structural and post-humanist theoretical frameworks. There are implications emerging for understanding
knowledge and truth as fragile, contested and contingent, encouraging
the production of locally situated knowledge and suggesting a place for
the application of professional learning methodologies that contribute
richly textured accounts of local action and their effects and to building local

leadership. A number of writers have highlighted the particular challenges for the field at a time when neo-liberal discourses of accountability and the dominance of human capital framings cut across the new imaginings and social transformational possibilities opened up by this flourishing of intellectual energy. According to Skattebol and Arthur (2014), the current times call for an adaptive leadership characterised by an activist professionalism in order to engage with government agendas and exercise moral judgement. They also argue that Fenech and Sumsion's (2007a, 2007b) empirical study on the impact of regulation on early childhood educators demonstrates the critical significance of the 'level of intellectual resources held by educators and the power they can galvanise in their professional identity' that enables them to forge the alliances and leverage community concerns that will enable them to make strategic representations and practise resistance to the dominant discourse. They make a cogent case that the practice of collaborative practitioner research can develop the kind of capabilities necessary for these professionals.

This new vibrancy in early childhood research, policy and practice to which we have gestured suggests a particular timeliness to articulating methodologies that can resource the further development of the locally activist 'critically reflective emotional professional' (Osgood, 2010: 119). By documenting and celebrating the experiences and achievements of practitioner research(ers) in early childhood contexts, this book provides compelling evidence of practitioner research as an appropriate approach to creating new situated and contextually relevant knowledge about the field and its contribution to growing the capacity of the profession.

The distinctiveness of practitioner research and its contributions

In this volume, practitioner research is used as an umbrella term for a wide range of approaches and methods to field research that are inquiry-based, concerned with gaining greater insight into, and strengthening, professional practice. These approaches have been variously called 'practitioner inquiry' (Cochran-Smith and Lytle, 2007), 'participatory action research' (Kapoor and Jordan, 2009), 'participatory research' (Olivier et al., 2009), 'action research' (Elliott, 2008; Noffke and Somekh, 2009; Somekh and Zeichner, 2009), 'applied and practice-based research' (Furlong and Oancea, 2005), 'practitioner research' (Groundwater-Smith and Mockler, 2008), 'teacher professional learning' (Gore et al., 2010), teacher research, self-study, narrative inquiry, or the scholarship of teaching and learning (Cochran-Smith and Lytle, 2007). Each carry their own epistemology and methods, and the terms are not necessarily interchangeable. These approaches build from the understanding that inquiry is a stance that researchers take, and in which the social, cultural and historical forces shaping and influencing this form of research are taken into account. Participants in such inquiry work in collaboration with others – university researchers, teachers and community activists, for example. Ethical imperatives are implicitly and explicitly a part of practitioner research and questions arise as to what 'scientific research' is. Critics of the approach, for example funding bodies and governing institutions, claim it is too subjective, unclear and lacking in measures of validity and reliability (Cochran-Smith and Lytle, 2007). Proponents, however, all advocate for its strong epistemological and theoretical underpinnings and argue that practitioners who hold significant knowledge from inside practice should be empowered as researchers of their own practice, allowing the most valid and sustainable change to be possible. Such an approach to systematic and intentional data collection, with analysis grounded in the context, holds the strongest potential for meaningful change (Cochrane-Smith and Lytle, 2007, 2009). For further reading see Campbell and Groundwater-Smith, 2007; Cochran-Smith and Donnell, 2006; Green et al., 2006.

The common features of practitioner research are what make it distinctive as a field and include involving practitioners as researchers, usually of their own practice; collaboration between different actors; the local community or sites of practice being the context for inquiry; knowledge being made open for scrutiny and new knowledge being created; a recognition that knowledge of worth needs to be created 'inside' rather than transported in from 'outside' (as in traditional staff development) and for immediate use; practitioners are 'knowers'; critical reflection on the theory–practice nexus; inquiry as an integral part of practice; and inquiry is systematic, intentional and reported (Cochran-Smith and Lytle, 2007). Typically practitioner researchers and academic researchers are partners, rather than research subject and researcher (researching 'with' rather than 'about'), often resulting in a transformation of existing relationships.

Advocates for practitioner research, and people who have engaged in this form of research and its variants (academic and field-based), talk of its shared features and assumptions across issues of power, its political nature, the potential to assist real and sustained change, authenticity and 'realness'.

Kemmis et al. (2014: 2) discuss their evolution as researchers in the following way:

> We have moved beyond thinking of action research as an approach to research and change which is best represented as a self-reflective spiral of cycles of planning, acting and observing, reflecting and then re-planning in successive cycles of improvement. We re-affirm that the purpose of critical participatory action research is to change social practices, including research practice itself, to make them more rational and reasonable, more productive and sustainable, and more just and inclusive.

There is no doubt that this form of research can be rigorous, complex and slow, is theorisable, and offers no 'easy way out' for researchers, although it renders the research process and relationships more visible and accessible. Experienced researchers in this field note the potential to realign power relationships, in which traditional knowledge–power relationships, such as those that exist between the academy and practitioners, are reconfigured. As a consequence of this experience, practitioners emerge with greater confidence in their ability to 'know' and to 'find out' (Cochran-Smith and Lytle, 2007). Teachers as researchers can construct a common tradition of understanding and knowledge based on their research and actions (Elliott, 2009).

In this book, the terms teacher research and practitioner research are used interchangeably. Our rationale is that not all of the people working with young children, families and communities are teachers. It is a more complex scenario than in schools where the adults are mostly teachers. Reading the chapters in the book will provide encounters with stories of teachers, educators with other qualifications from the vocational education and training sector, family members and community members who have all participated in practitioner research in some way. Practitioner research is seen as a legitimate method in reshaping this divide between teachers and academics, with one distinction being that teachers are very likely to be involved in some capacity. Like the other methods described here, practitioner research is a deeply ethical undertaking with implications for confidentiality, transparency and truly informed consent during methodological planning and application phases. Teacher/practitioner research is 'grounded fundamentally in the dialectic of inquiry and practice rather than in one particular theoretical tradition and envisions the teacher as a knower, rather than a technician. The dialectic is viewed as an integrated process involving reciprocity, research and practice relationships, analysis, action and theorising' (Cochran-Smith and Lytle, 2009: 42). For further reading see Gore and Gitlin, 2004.

Creation of locally situated knowledge

Hegemonic discourses abound in education and early childhood contexts, giving rise to the notion that there is one (typically western, or northern) way of interpreting the world, for example, of being a 'good' teacher, or of providing quality teaching and learning environments. Practitioner research provides the frameworks, tools and processes for investigating these knowledge claims in local sites and can be enabling of the production of new knowledge that is contextually relevant and may differ from the orthodox wisdom. This aspect of local knowledge production takes on heightened significance in contexts of cultural and ethnic diversity and in high poverty and socially disadvantaged communities. Typically these communities experience marginalisation and social exclusion when the institutional policy and practices are shaped only by the hegemonic knowledge discourse. Through the implementation of practitioner research, the subjugated knowledges of minority and excluded groups can be brought forward and used to show how different policies and practices might advance equity, social justice and social inclusion.

Collaboration

Research involving practitioners and academic researchers as partners is now quite widely practised in education contexts (e.g. Cochran-Smith and Lytle, 2007) and health research (Olivier et al., 2009) and has marked a shift in the relationships between sites of practice and the academy. In education contexts this shift is not unproblematic though, either for practitioners or academics.

Invariably, practitioner research, in whatever form it comes, becomes a political act of claiming power and agency for the practitioners, who usually have not had this in the past. There is an important aspect of self-determination involved and an intent to shift the status quo frequently emerges. This can be challenging for schools and universities (Cochran-Smith and Lytle, 2007). Olivier et al. (2009: 13) attribute this to the active participation of practitioners as they 'identify issues and ways of dealing with them' within an enabling methodology that promotes social action. Participants can identify their own community strengths and challenges, engage in dialogue, decide for themselves what is important and what needs to be changed, and engage the wider community.

This is illustrated when Skattebol and Arthur (2014) write about their experience as academic partners in a practitioner research project in Sydney, drawing on the theorisations of Bhabha (1994) to conceptualise the changed dynamics and relationships as a new 'third space' in which the production of contextually relevant knowledge can take place, without which this kind of collaboration is often not possible due to the siloing of institutional knowledge and practices.

Variants of practitioner research

Space does not allow the provision of detailed outlines of various methods in this volume, and these are well covered elsewhere (see, for example, Cochran-Smith and Lytle, 2009). Readers will find variations on a range of practitioner research methods described in detail in each of the following chapters. However, a brief description of two well-regarded variations, action research, and practitioner action research (PAR) are included here.

Action research

Action research has a long and proud tradition in community projects of social change and in education (Kemmis et al., 2014). It is mostly identified as a spiralling cycle containing phases of choosing to change, planning for a change, creating change and sharing the lessons of change. It is based on principles of reflexive adult learning (MacNaughton and Hughes, 2009). It is not, however, reducible to 'public scholarship', but a process that 'engages simultaneous understanding of social action as a way to produce reliable theories, methods and knowledge' (Denzin and Lincoln, 2011: 30). Kemmis et al. (2014) claim its strengths lie in rejecting conventional expert-led research; the recognition of capacity by participants at every step in the research; and a participant-led orientation to making improvements in practices. It is not without its critics, however, who claim that it makes few contributions to theoretical and methodological debates in the social sciences. Case reporting is seen to lack sharp intellectual focus and be unlinked to a scientific discourse. Critics draw attention to a lack of integration between solving relevant practical problems and well developed theoretical and methodological agenda (Denzin and Lincoln, 2011: 30). However, there is considerable resonance in this volume with Somekh and Zeichner's strong advocacy for action research that, 'Action research, as a proposition, has discursive power because it embodies a collision of terms. In generating research knowledge and improving social action at the same time, action research challenges the normative values of two distinct ways of being – that of the scholar and the activist' (2009: 5). For further reading see Elliott, 2008; Maksimovic, 2011; Mockler, 2007; and Newman and Mowbray, 2012.

Participatory Action Research (PAR)

While all practitioner and action research has political intentions to some extent, Participatory Action Research (PAR) is characterised by its political nature and political interests. There is argument that PAR should be returned to its longstanding anti-colonial roots and indigenous traditions from Latin-America where it has a close relationship with critical pedagogy and democratic participatory rights. It recognises that educators, particularly in poor schools, are often powerless, and carries an emancipatory vision (Darder, 2011). It follows the work of Paulo Freire and rests on the assumption that participation in the past has been largely repressed by the state, and needs to move into morally authentic, rather than simulated, participation (Flores-Kastanis et al., 2009). For further reading see Kapoor and Jordan, 2009.

Practitioner research in early childhood contexts: building a repository of practitioner research knowledge

The defining focus for this volume has been to assemble a range of practitioner research projects 'put to work' in very diverse early childhood contexts, bringing forward insights related to choices of methodology, implementation and their contribution to practice while rendering understandable the different approaches adopted and how these were inflected in particular contexts. The resulting chapters profile a rich array of approaches to collaborative practitioner research in extremely diverse contexts including urban, regional and remote areas across the northern and southern hemispheres and in different parts of the world (South Africa, Scandinavia, Chile and Australia). While the particular focus of each chapter varies, each one includes a description of the research context, outlines the practitioner research methodology adopted for the project, and highlights research findings, particularly as these relate to the particular contribution, challenges and outcomes of the project. A number of themes emerge from these strands, and it is through these themes that we choose to introduce the book chapters: constructing collaborative relationships, knowledge and knowing, capacity building and transformation and change. Of course these themes are interwoven across the chapters, and what emerges is indeed a 'rich tapestry' of practitioner research experiences.

The final chapter is by guest author Dr Nicole Mockler and her research partner Ashley Casey – '(In)sights from 40 years of practitioner action research in education: perspectives from the US, UK and Australia'. Nicole was invited into this book in recognition of her widely respected work in practitioner research in schools over a sustained period and her authorship of highly regarded writings about teacher research in schools. Nicole provides insights for early childhood professionals from this extensive work with practitioner research over many years, and together with Ashley provides insights about its inflection in local sites through the use of an insider/outsider perspective. This reflects the ethos of both the book and also of practitioner research, and contributes to the book's messages of authenticity, collaboration and 'groundedness'. Most of the chapters are co-authored by practitioners and their academic partners, with time taken to establish how these relationships were formed and enacted.

Constructing collaborative partnerships

Across the chapters, the forms of collaboration and the roles of the collaborators are seen to differ according to the context of the different settings and variations in the practitioner research methodology utilised. The importance of deeply respectful relationships to successful research collaborations is powerfully demonstrated in the context of a transnational project, which is the focus of Chapter 2, 'Collaborative capacity building in early childhood communities in Chile'. Here the authors, Linda Newman and Christine Woodrow, from Australia, and Chilean educators Silvia Rójo and Mónica Galvez, describe how challenges to current practices brought about through the intervention of the Futuro Infantil Hoy project were constructively addressed through the development of trusting reciprocal relationships. This occurred through their joint engagement in sociocultural theory, iterative cycles of action research, and new forms of practitioner research involving photostories. The chapter illustrates the growth of these relationships and the blurring and changing roles as the practitioners took on expanded leadership roles within the project as they and the academic partners came together in the joint project of writing the chapter. Similarly, Chapter 7, 'Sustaining curriculum renewal in Western Sydney: three participant views' by Linda Newman, Janet Keegan and Trish Heeley, draws our attention to how roles evolved over the course of the project and lead to the academic partner moving from facilitator to partner and one of the practitioner researchers moving to a leadership role in the context of the Curriculum Renewal Group implemented in a large municipality in Western Sydney. The chapter allows us to see how the experiences in the initial cycles provided a foundation for evolving a sustained model of enhanced collaboration across the sites of the project. Collaborative relationships are also fundamental to the success of the Sharing Care project in South Africa, beautifully articulated through the voices of the practitioner Mary Janes and academic partner Norma Rudolph in Chapter 6, 'Reconceptualising services for young children through dialogue in a South African village'. Collaborative community engagement also emerged as crucial to the success of this project.

Knowledge and knowing

All of the chapters describe cases in which the research involved a collaborative partnership between the academy and the sites of practice, and several of these showed transformations in the knowledge–power relationships in the partnerships, and the repositioning of practitioners as agentic knowers. This latter point about agentic knowing is most powerfully demonstrated in this volume in Chapter 3, 'Insider Islamic spaces of inquiry: Muslim educators producing new knowledge in Sydney Australia', by Oznur Ayedimir, Fatima Mourad, Leonie Arthur and Jen Skattebol. The chapter describes how a group of Muslim early childhood practitioners in Australia (calling themselves the *Habibties*) adopted practitioner research to investigate how professional identities were constructed and reconstructed by Muslim educators working across Muslim and secular educational institutions under the pressures of Islamophobia. It provides powerful insights into how practitioner research supported them in 'rescuing' and reconstructing marginalised Islamic informed pedagogical knowledge. The co-authors use the term 'epistemic disobedience' to describe the point at which the practitioner research processes enabled the negotiation of dissonance and their resistance to hegemonic and stereotypical knowledge regimes. Reformulating and formalising existing knowledge into new frameworks to support a quality focus was an important outcome from the project described in Chapter 5, 'Developing collaboration using mind maps in practitioner research in Sweden' by Karin Rönnerman. Here the academic partner, Karin, led a collaborative inquiry process in which the practitioners investigated and made sense of their practice through the use of a mind-mapping tool. The tool itself fostered collaboration using action research constructed within a long-standing Nordic tradition of study circles. The chapter details the processes used in developing the mind map in ways that deepened the participants' knowledge of their curriculum practice, in order that it might be changed, and how this occurred is also part of the research presented in the chapter.

Continuing the theme of reclaiming marginalised knowledge through collaborative practitioner research is Chapter 4, 'What is play for, in your culture? Investigating remote Australian Aboriginal perspectives through participatory practitioner research' by Lyn Fasoli and Alison Wunungmurra. The project focuses on remote Aboriginal community perspectives of play and involves children as researchers of their own play to make important culturally relevant knowledge visible-knowledge. It had previously been invisible and seemingly unknowable because of the dominance of hegemonic white knowledge about children's play. Fundamental to the research relationship was also the notion of authentic reciprocity in the relationships so that both Alison, the aboriginal researcher, and Lyn, the white academic, could gain differentiated knowledge and insights from the project. The authors help us understand the fragility of these relationships and the importance of respect and reciprocity in sustaining them.

Capacity building

All of the chapters provide insights into how practitioner research approaches build capacity as knowers and as actors. The importance and outcomes from this are especially highlighted in the context of the appreciative enquiry approach adopted in the South African context of the HIV/AIDS pandemic and a discourse of children's rights. The authors present a vivid account of how the appreciative enquiry supported building community ownership of change and how critical this was to improving children's life chances. Chapter 2 about Futuro Infantil Hoy and Chapter 5 about the mind-mapping project also illustrate the capacity building dimension of practitioner research: in the Chile context, practitioners becoming leaders and authors, and in Chapter 5 deeper knowers and thinkers in action research, mind-mapping and collaborating. Chapter 7 also provides evidence of a much more robust professional community in the Curriculum Renewal Group because of the way the project evolved, leadership shifted, and iterative cycles informed the next cycle to be more participative. The sustainability of this project seems well founded now.

Transformation and change

Transformation is a big claim and one that many are loath to identify with. However, the vibrancy of the writing in these chapters provides the reader with a sense that every project contained an element of personal, collective or institutional transformation, or a combination. Reviewing the chapters, overall, we can sense that each of the authors are powerful advocates for practitioner research, not the least because of the positive changes that its use has wrought.

Conclusions and insights gained

This chapter has charted some of the territory of practitioner research, providing a broad framework for understanding, learning from and enjoying the work presented in this volume, at the same time making a case for why practitioner research has an important place and contribution to make in the field of early childhood research and why it should be more strongly articulated as a powerful methodology for the field to take up. It remains now for readers to engage with the chapters and make their own meanings from the authors' presentation of their research experiences in all their vibrancy, richness and complexity.

References

Bhabha, H. K. (ed.) (1994) *The Location of Culture*. London: Routledge.

Bown, K., Sumsion, J. and Press, F. (2009) 'Influences on politicians' decision making for early childhood education and care policy: what do we know? What don't we know?', *Contemporary Issues in Early Childhood*, 10 (3): 194–217.

Campbell, A. and Groundwater-Smith, S. (eds) (2007) *An Ethical Approach to Practitioner Research: Dealing with Issues*. Hokoben, NY: Routledge.

Cochran-Smith, M. and Donnell, K. (2006) 'Practitioner inquiry: blurring the boundaries of research and practice', in J. L. Green, G. Camilli and P. B. Elmore (eds), *Handbook of Complementary Methods in Education Research*. Washington: AERA and Mahwah, NJ: Erlbaum, pp.503–18.

Cochran-Smith, M. and Lytle, S. (2007) 'Everything's ethics: practitioner inquiry and university culture', in A. Campbell and S. Groundwater-Smith (eds), *An Ethical Approach to Practitioner Research: Dealing with Issues*. Hokoben, NY: Routledge, pp. 24–41.

Cochran-Smith, M. and Lytle, S. (2009) 'Teacher research as stance', in S. Noffke and B. Somekh (eds), *The Sage Handbook of Educational Action Research*. London: Sage, pp. 39–49.

Dahlberg, G., Moss, P. and Pence, A. (2007) *Beyond Quality in Early Childhood Education and Care: Languages of Evaluation*. London: Routledge, Taylor and Francis.

Darder, A. (2011) *A Dissident Voice: Essays on Culture, Pedagogy and Power*. New York: Peter Lang.

Denzin, N. and Lincoln, Y. (2011) *The Sage Handbook of Qualitative Research* (4th edn). Thousand Oaks, CA: Sage.

Elliott, J. (2007) 'A Curriculum for the Study of Human Affairs: the Contribution of Lawrence Stenhouse' in J. Elliott (Ed.), *Reflecting where the action is: The selected works of John Elliott*. London: Routledge.

Elliott, J. (2008) 'Assessing the quality of action research', in J. Furlong and A. Oancea (eds), *Assessing Quality in Applied Practice-based Research in Education*. Abingdon: Routledge, pp. 110–26.

Elliott, J. (2009) 'Building educational theory through action research', in S. Noffke and B. Somekh (eds), *The Sage Handbook of Educational Action Research*. London: Sage, pp. 28–38.

Fenech, M. and Sumsion, J. (2007a) 'Early childhood teachers and regulation: complicating power relations using a Foucauldian lens', *Contemporary Issues in Early Childhood*, 8 (2): 109–22.

Fenech, M. and Sumsion, J. (2007b) 'Promoting high quality early childhood education and care services: beyond risk management, performative constructions of regulation', *Journal of Early Childhood Research*, 5 (2): 263–83.

Fenech, M., Sumsion, J. and Goodfellow, J. (2006) 'The regulatory environment in long day care: a "double-edged sword" for early childhood professional practice', *Australian Journal of Early Childhood*, 5 (1): 194–217.

Fenech, M., Sumsion, J. and Goodfellow, J. (2008) 'Regulation and risk: early childhood education and care services as sites where "the laugh of Foucault" resounds', *Journal of Education Policy*, 23 (1): 35–48.

Flores-Kastanis, E., Montoya-Vargas, J. and Suárez, D. (2009) 'Participatory action research in Latin-American education: a road map to a different part of the world', in S. Noffke and B. Somekh (eds), *The Sage Handbook of Educational Action Research*. London: Sage, pp. 453–66.

Furlong, J. and Oancea, A. (2005) *Assessing Quality in Applied and Practice-based Educational Research: A Framework for Discussion*. Oxford University Department of Educational Studies. Retrieved from: www.tlrp.org/capacity/rm/wt/campbell/docs/assessing_quality_shortreport_tcm6-8232.pdf (last accessed 9 December 2014).

Gore, J., Bowe, J. and Elsworth, W. (2010) 'Examining the impact of quality teaching rounds on teacher professional learning', paper presented at the Australian Association of Research in Education (AARE) International Education Research Conference, Melbourne. Retrieved from: www.aare.edu.au/confpap.htm (last accessed 8 December 2014).

Gore, J. and Gitlin, A. (2004) '[Re]Visioning the academic-teacher divide: Power and knowledge in the educational community', *Teachers and Teaching: Theory and Practice*, 10 (1): 35–58.

Green, J., Camilli, G. and Elmore, P. (2006) *Handbook of Complementary Methods in Education Research*. Washington: AERA and Mahwah, NJ: Erlbaum.

Groundwater-Smith, S. and Mockler, N. (2008) 'Ethics in practitioner research: an issue of quality', in J. Furlong and A. Oancea (eds), *Assessing Quality in Applied and Practice-Based Research in Education*. Abingdon: Routledge, pp. 79–92.

Kapoor, D. and Jordan, S. (eds) (2009) *Education, Participatory Action Research and Social Change: International Perspectives*. New York: Palgrave MacMillan.

Kemmis, S., McTaggart, R. and Nixon, R. (2014). *The Action Research Planner. Doing Critical Participatory Action Research*. Singapore: Springer.

MacNaughton, G. and Hughes, P. (2009) *Doing Action Research in Early Childhood Studies*. Berkshire: Open University Press.

Maksimovic, J. A. S. (2011) 'Researcher–practitioner's role in action research', *Androgogic Perspectives*, June (2): 54–62.

Miller, L. (2008). 'Developing professionalism within a regulatory framework in England: Challenges and possibilities', *European Early Childhood Education Research Journal*, 16(2): 255–269.

Mitchell, L. and Cubey, P. (2003) *Characteristics of Professional Development Linked to Enhanced Pedagogy and Children's Learning in Early Childhood Settings: Best Evidence Synthesis*. New Zealand: Ministry of Education.

Mockler, N. (2007) 'Ethics in practitioner research: dilemmas from the field', in A. Campbell and S. Groundwater-Smith (eds), *An Ethical Approach to Practitioner Research*. New York: Routledge, pp. 88–99.

Moss, P. (2007) 'Meetings across the paradigmatic divide', *Educational Philosophy and Theory*, 39 (3): 229–45.

Moss, P. (2012) *Early Childhood and Compulsory Education: Reconceptualising the Relationship*. London. Routledge.

Moyles, J. (2001) 'Passion, paradox and professionalism in the early years education', *Early Years: Journal of International Research and Development*, 21 (2): 81–95. DOI: 10.1080/09575140124792.

Newman, L. and Mowbray, S. (2012) '"We were expected to be equal": teachers and academics sharing professional learning through practitioner inquiry', *Teachers and Teaching: Theory and Practice*, 18 (4): 455–68.

Noffke, S. and Somekh, B. (2009) (eds) *The Sage Handbook of Educational Action Research*. London: Sage.

Olivier, T., Wood, L. and de Lange, N. (2009) *Picturing Hope in the Face of Poverty as Seen through the Eyes of Teachers: Photovoice – A Research Methodology*. Cape Town: Juta and Company (Pty) Ltd.

Osgood, J. (2006) 'Deconstructing professionalism in early childhood education: resisting the regulatory gaze', *Contemporary Issues in Early Childhood*, 7 (1): 5–16.

Osgood, J. (2010) 'Reconstructing professionalism in ECEC: the case for the "critically reflective emotional professional"', *Early Years: An International Research Journal*, 30 (2): 119–33.

Pardo, M. and Woodrow, C. (2014) 'Strengthening early childhood education in Chile: tensions between public policy and teacher discourses over the schoolarisation of early childhood education professional identity', *International Journal of Early Childhood*, 46 (1): 101–15. DOI: 10.1007/s13158-014-0102-0.

Skattebol, J. and Arthur, L. (2014) 'Collaborative practitioner research: opening a third space for local knowledge production', *Asia Pacific Journal of Education*, 34 (3): 351–65.

Somekh, B. and Zeichner, K. (2009) 'Action research for educational reform: remodelling action research theories and practices in local contexts', *Educational Action Research*, 17 (1): 5–21.

Sumsion, J., Barnes, S., Cheeseman, S., Harrison, L., Kennedy, A. and Stonehouse, A. (2009) 'Insider perspectives on developing belonging, being and becoming: the Early Years Learning Framework for Australia', *Australian Journal of Early Childhood*, 34 (4): 4–13.

Taggart, J. (2011) 'Don't we care? The ethics and emotional labour of early years professionalism', *Early Years: An International Research Journal*, 31 (1): 85–95.

Vescio, V., Ross, D. and Adams, A. (2008) 'A review of research on the impact of professional learning communities on teaching practice and student learning', *Teaching and Teacher Education*, 24: 80–91.

Woodrow, C. (2011) 'Challenging identities: a case for leadership', in L. Miller and C. Cable (eds), *Professionalism, Leadership and Management*, London: Sage, pp. 29–46.

Woodrow, C. and Brennan, M. (1999) 'Marketised positioning of early childhood education: new contexts for curriculum and professional development in Queensland, Australia', *Contemporary Issues in Early Childhood*, 1 (1): 79–95.

2

COLLABORATIVE CAPACITY BUILDING IN EARLY CHILDHOOD COMMUNITIES IN CHILE

Linda Newman, Christine Woodrow,
Silvia Rójo and Mónica Galvez

Key words practitioner research; pedagogical change; collaborative research; action research; community capacity building.

Chapter overview

The focus of this chapter is the engagement of the four co-authors in a cross-national action research project called Futuro Infantil Hoy (FIH) developed in Chile by Chilean early childhood centre-based educators and Australian university-based researchers. It describes how co-authors Mónica and Silvia collaborated as co-researchers with Linda and Christine, and played an active leadership role in the iterative processes involved in developing the project, suggesting and informing each subsequent phase of action and researching the process. The chapter records a culminating cycle of practitioner research and is particularly concerned with Sylvia and Mónica's perspectives about their own learning and change.

By documenting how we worked together as experienced and new researchers and revealing the responses, feelings and actions of the practitioner researchers we hope to provide insights into what is at

(Continued)

(Continued)

stake when educators enter into collaborative relationships with others and transform themselves as practitioner researchers. Our key themes include the explicit socioculturally informed epistemological and ontological beliefs introduced by the Australian team and the implications of these for collaborations in practitioner research. Other key themes are the collaboration and capacity building embedded in the project and the way the Australian researchers therefore adopted an ongoing reflective action research frame, aiming to avoid the pitfalls associated with being positioned as 'experts'.

Readers will see how the use of a thoughtfully chosen theoretical framing can inform, guide and give meaning to their own practitioner research. They can see how sustainable change can be planned, implemented, extended and embedded into practice, strengthening both planning and outcomes of practitioner research. These insights may be helpful for educators planning their own practitioner research projects.

Rationale and aims

A key aim of the FIH project was to explore the use of practitioner research as a vehicle for productive collaborative pedagogical change. As a research team of academics and classroom educators we aimed to understand our changing participation in the sociocultural activity of our shared and evolving community of learners (Rogoff, 2003), to reflect on our own learning and better understand issues related to the project in which we all worked.

The research considered questions of what it meant for practitioners in early childhood education in Antofagasta, Chile to learn about, understand and implement sociocultural approaches in their pedagogical practice through the following questions:

- What does it mean personally, interpersonally and in the community for practitioner researchers to implement a sociocultural approach to early childhood curriculum in Antofagasta, Chile?
- To what extent can sociocultural approaches be made accessible, understandable and engaging for a group of Chilean educators?
- How are sociocultural approaches and concepts, introduced by a foreign university, adapted and taken up in local sites?
- What are the benefits and challenges in re-forming existing practices and adopting new approaches?

These issues are centrally important in building deeper understandings about factors implicated in mobilising pedagogical change, and the significant ways socioculturally informed practitioner research approaches might contribute to improving the quality of children's and practitioners' learning, enhancing family involvement and addressing inequalities deriving from children's experience of living in social disadvantage. Of additional interest is how to promote social justice within democratic values 'in a more equal, participative and inclusive' practice in order that children may be seen as 'social actors and citizens in society' (Galdames, 2011: 120). In doing this we respond to Alexander's call for a greater emphasis on pedagogical processes in writing about cross-national work, to come a little closer to understanding the themes of curriculum, pedagogic styles and evaluation which contribute to forming identities in education and emphasise the process of learning itself (Alexander, 2001).

Christine and Linda's interest is in how practitioner research conducted within university–practitioner partnerships can create strong, ongoing professional relationships that lead to sustainable change. Silvia and Mónica's intention is to make their work visible, and in Mónica's case, honour the achievements in her centre. Both say they are realising a dream by taking on identities as co-authors.

The chapter begins with a brief outline showing how our working relationship evolved. This is followed by a description of the research project that provided the context and framework for the centre-based practitioner research and the sociopolitical context in which the overall project was conceived, followed by an exploration of the theoretical framings of the project. The methodology and methods are outlined and finally, in response to the research questions, the findings of Silvia and Mónica's exposés of their respective research journeys are shared. We conclude by discussing our thoughts about our shared socioculturally informed learning journey.

How the authors came to be working together

FIH began as an initiative of the Chilean government under its reform agenda to improve the quality of early childhood education. It developed as a collaboration between the private sector (Fundación Minera Escondida (FME)), an Australian university, the government and Chilean early childhood service providers to design and implement a pedagogical change project in very disadvantaged communities in the northern Chilean city of Antofagasta.

Silvia is Chilean and was an early childhood classroom educator and centre director when she joined the project. She is now a *mentora* (mentor) working for FME in the ongoing expansion of the project. Mónica is a Chilean early childhood classroom educator and centre director, employed by a large early childhood agency in Chile and now an FIH centre-based *mentora*. Christine and Linda are Australian academics who had previous experience working together in projects reconceptualising early childhood teacher education through sociocultural perspectives in communities of practice (Ashton and Newman, 2006; Newman and Ashton, 2009; Newman and Woodrow, 2007). They were both previously early childhood teachers.

Through FIH, the Australian team partnered with Chilean educators, including Silvia and Mónica's teams, in a programme of pedagogical innovation and change to learn about the application of practitioner research, sociocultural theory and literacy pedagogies. This took place within a professional learning programme later described in the chapter in which educators undertook a series of practitioner research projects. Silvia and Mónica report here on their roles in action research cycles over the two-year pilot period. Readers can see how we have moved through stages of being research leaders/ participants, co-researchers, and now collaborating authors of this chapter.

Description of the study

The FIH project was situated in a regional area characterised by the contrasting landscape of rapid growth, high poverty and social disadvantage. Antofagasta is a copper mining port city in the far north of Chile on the edge of the driest desert on earth, the Atacama, with a population of approximately 360,000. It has the highest GDP per capita for Chile and, at the same time, extreme poverty exacerbated by unemployment, drug use and illegal immigration. It has the widest discrepancy in educational outcomes in the country (Antofagasta, n.d.). Poverty levels of up to 50 per cent are reported in some regions. Inequality in salaries is high and public expenditure is low. Poverty in the region averages at 7 per cent (Parra and Franks, 2011). Significant social problems are evident as a result of the inequalities.

Silvia explains that Antofagasta is a very expensive city to live in and life can be really hard for lower income earners, in particular those living in poverty. Although it is true that many families earn well, families often disintegrate and she observes how high earning is associated with a high floating population, with many coming to work in the mining industry to send money to their families.

Chile's well-documented history of hierarchical decentralised institutionality and governance (Umayahara, 2006) has contributed to early childhood educators and managers experiencing professional isolation and having little or no experience of cross-institutional interaction or collaboration. FIH provided opportunities for educators to network and collaborate across institutions for the first time in their professional lives.

Mónica explains that previously there was no communication and no desire to communicate between centres and institutions. She wanted to tell other centres about FIH but her institution didn't give her the opportunity to do so.

Professional learning through action research

The FIH project began as a three-year pilot in five sites (early childhood centres and transition classes in schools). It aimed to strengthen children's learning, and increase the meaningful involvement of families in their children's learning through engaging educators in deep professional learning. These aims were operationalised through the development of the Literacy Connections: Linking Children, Families and Communities professional learning programme (workshops, readings and classroom support) and Leadership Round Tables (LRTs). Literacy Connections is a literacy focused community capacity building programme built around a series of action research cycles supported by new learning from sociocultural perspectives. It incorporated reflection on changes in centres in collaboration between Chilean and Australian colleagues. Following workshops where new sociocultural concepts such as 'funds of knowledge' (Gonzalez et al., 2005), literacy as social practice (Perry, 2012), co-construction, child agency and pedagogical documentation were introduced, participants implemented new ideas in their classrooms as they saw fit. Additionally directors and lead educators learned about communities of practice, pedagogical leadership, community leadership, action research, use of an early childhood environment rating scale, supported playgroups and digital storytelling in LRTs.

Methodology

Research in FIH has largely focused on investigating what it means to collaborate for pedagogical change across different time, culture, heritage and language. In a context where research has generated substantial evidence about the positive impact and outcomes from the pilot (Woodrow et al., 2014), we are now building deeper understandings in this chapter about the factors implicated in mobilising pedagogical change, and the significant ways sociocultural approaches might contribute to improving the quality of children's learning, enhance family involvement, and address inequalities deriving from children's experience of living in social disadvantage. We are also seeking to better understand how practitioner research and academic/educator projects can lead to sustainable professional learning and how long-term educational and social change can be, as Silvia desires, 'a force in education'. Selecting appropriate methodology involves choosing the best approaches for acquiring and activating knowledge (Denzin and

Lincoln, 2013). It necessarily embeds choices about the theoretical framings that inform those choices. Our methodological choices then needed to be consistent with FIH's explicit sociocultural framing and practitioner research suited to that imperative.

Working within a sociocultural approach

Sociocultural theory and associated approaches to pedagogy and working with families were key and explicit conceptual framings of FIH. While recognising that 'in the field of early childhood education and develop-ment we find a polyphonic chorus of methodological voices' (Fleer, 2014: 4), increasingly, sociocultural approaches are gaining prominence in early childhood contexts, gradually replacing the dominance of develop-mentalism (Veresov, 2014). We are conscious in our choice of theoretical positioning that learners and their interaction with their social environ-ment are best suited to the cultural-social-historical context of our work (Gray and MacBlain, 2012). It is less common that sociocultural theory is adopted to explore and document the experience of educators and researchers themselves than for work with children, and the approach was new to FIH participants as their curriculum is strongly framed by dis-courses of developmentalism, which are increasingly recognised as being essentialist and reducing children's lives to a series of predictable stages rather than as living within relationships (Galdames, 2011; Veresov, 2014). As with any change of approach there were implications for re-framing the understandings and practices for children's families, communities and educators (Pennington et al., 2013). For the Chilean educators this pro-vided opportunities for choices about 'cultural borrowings' (Alexander, 2001), in order to decide which of the offered concepts and practices may be useful to their cultural-historical contexts.

Sociocultural approaches are characterised by an emphasis on the role of contextual, cultural and historical influences on the development of learning within their communities. Linda and Christine saw potential in the co-constructive approaches of sociocultural theory for work with local educators in the Chilean context, as they both rejected culturally irrelevant 'quick fix' literacy strategies for short-term change that often characterise literacy interventions. For children, sociocultural approaches embed a shift away from the dominant views of early learning as predictable and located within the individual. Broader views, recognising the social and contextual nature of development and learning are proposed by Vygotsky (1978) and Rogoff among others. Rogoff (1998) conceptualised learning within three planes: firstly, the individual; secondly, relations between individuals and rela-tions between the individual and others/interpersonal; and thirdly, learning within organisational/community settings (Rogoff, n.d.). We have addressed these dimensions in our programme of research. This has required recognition that a major aspect of planning for young children's and adults' learning involves interactions with people and agencies other than those within the early childhood centre and the adoption of learning-based interactions by all adults with children, irrespective of training level. This approach, in which Silvia and Mónica shared leadership, has questioned and challenged the dominant universal (Eurocentric) and embedded approaches to early childhood curriculum that were evident in practice in the Chilean centres as outlined in the 'curricular framework' (Galdames, 2011). Children's learning was typically separate from the contexts and experiences of their daily lives, creating barriers to families' understanding of their children's learning. Teaching and learning was traditionally the remit of teachers only, not the other adults (assistants) in the centre, and meaningful connections with families were rare in an embedded and taken-for-granted knowledge transfer structure that in Galdames' view 'reaffirms the colonialist ideology of the past' (2011: 115). This comes about because, despite 'freedom of teaching promoted in [the Organic Constitutional Law of Education]', there are contradictory messages because of having 'to respond to standards of service and enrolment rates while implementing statutory EC national curriculum' (Galdames, 2011: 115).

Practitioner research

The research described in this chapter can be seen both as multilayered and ongoing, centred on, and radiating from a core cycle of research. In one chapter it is impossible to outline this totality and that has not been our intention. Here we relate theoretical understandings and processes from culminating research that occurred within a greater whole. The FIH project was planned as action research that drew on the philosophies and values of practitioner research. Here we have drawn on Cochran-Smith and Lytle's conceptualisation of 'teacher research', but thoughtfully chose the word practitioner rather than teacher to describe our particular approach and participants. The authors of this chapter are all teachers, but not all those with whom we worked are. We see practitioner research as a process of learning to teach and lead within inquiry communities and through a long-term process. We see it as dialectic thinking and doing (Cochran-Smith and Lytle, 2007).

Supporting practitioner research with visual methodology: photostories as data

Typically data collection for practitioner research in education sites is gathered through observations and surveys. However, the developing field of visual research methodology has provided alternatives that serve practitioner research well. To assist the insider/outsider communication in the project we have used visual methodologies, inspired by the work of visual anthropologists (Pink, 2005, 2013) and in particular we discuss photostories here as method as well as mediating tool. Photostories as method involves the purposeful selection of photos, accompanied by an interpretive written narrative. Using photostories to represent learning, change and achievements, Silvia and Mónica were able to make their journeys accessible to insiders and outsiders together, with less reliance on the verbal in a context of negotiating two-way translations between English and Spanish. We did not work with 'found' or pre-existing images as many researchers do, but with images specifically generated during the research process to document and showcase change. Elsewhere we have discussed images produced by the Australian researchers (Newman et al., 2014), but here, the images used have been generated by Silvia and Mónica. The photostories helped answer the research questions by allowing the production of images that represented the dialectic of the learning process (Fleer, 2014). Photo images, however, are not transparent views into the centre, they interpret that world and display it in a particular way. The images are not used merely to illustrate something in the text, but are research data in their own right, 'unique sources of evidence' (Rose, 2007: 238). In this instance, the accompanying text from the photostories has been woven throughout the chapter as well as selected excerpts being shown to illustrate the data analysis process.

Method of data collection

Direct data generation for this chapter involved Silvia and Mónica initially being invited to produce a photostory reflection of their key changes one year on from the finish of the pilot. Guidelines were developed by the Australian team with the explicit goal of scaffolding them to prepare a succinct photostory to capture their own view of their key achievements. They each developed two sets of three photos, the first chosen to represent a key incident/feeling/image/representation of 'how it was' prior to, or at the beginning of the project, followed by a second set from the current time. These photos were used to elicit their writing about their experiences during the programme and after its completion. They were then asked to write 600 words of description and reflection that explained and analysed the photos using a set of guidelines. This was followed by a series of conversational interviews and email exchanges.

The methodological approach adopted to analyse the visual and textual data is a reflexive empirical one whereby we have shifted focus from the empirical data itself to 'as far as possible, a consideration of the perceptual, cognitive, theoretical, linguistic (inter) textual, political and cultural circumstances that form the backdrop to – as well as impregnate – the interpretations' (Alvesson and Sköldberg, 2009: 9). We are adopting a collaborative abductive approach to our data interpretation, which is in reality, the method most often used in practice where the empirical area of application is developed and the theory (the hypothetic over-arching pattern) is successively shifted and refined (Alvesson and Sköldberg, 2009).

Data analysis

The starting point for our socioculturally informed analysis is shown in the matrix in Table 2.1. Data analysis began with sorting the recorded evidence according to the matrix themes derived from Rogoff (1998, 2003), and then using collaborative abductive processes to develop understandings from the data, considering the perceptual, cognitive, theoretical, (inter) textual, political and cultural contexts to inform interpretation.

Our guiding theories and questions described earlier guide and ground our analysis (Moje et al., 2004). Written data were initially 'chunked' by phrase or 'natural unit of meaning' (Cohen et al., 2007: 470), and coded to identify author and chunk number. Photo narratives were coded using a different colour to distinguish them from interview narratives. Following this, units of meaning were organised into the matrix (Table 2.1) to note gestalts (patterns or themes) (Cohen et al., 2007). Although Cohen, Manion and Morrison caution about losing the holism and synergy of the data by fragmenting it, they also find it a useful way of moving from specific to the general and finding 'causal chains, networks and matrices' (2007: 470) that require researcher judgement.

As the project evolves, so too do we, and so temporality must be considered in writing and reading these data. As this chapter is in part constituted by original conversations between the authors, the chapter writing process itself also becomes further data in 'narrative time' with 'meaningful totalities'

Table 2.1 Sociocultural data analysis matrix (adapted from Edwards, 2006 and Rogoff, 1998, 2003, n.d.)

	Historical issues	Cultural issues	Contextual issues
Individual			
Interpersonal			
Community/ institutional change			

created out of separate events (Alvesson and Sköldberg, 2009: 128). The writing process has involved many face-to-face and online conversations, shared written narratives, interviews and transfers of the evolving chapter between countries. Multiple layers of translation have taken place to ensure that all authors fully understand each other in their respective first languages (Spanish and English).

Problems and challenges

Recognising the potential risks of replicating well-documented hierarchies of (Western) knowledge (Galdames, 2011) in such a complex undertaking, the overall project was carefully framed within a research and practice paradigm in which knowledge was treated as contestable, provisional and contextual and this has also played out during the writing of this chapter. This attempt to recognise and acknowledge multiple realities, we argue, contributed to a self-conscious reflexivity on the part of the Australian researchers, which positioned them as learners in a new cultural context along with their educator co-researchers, and as transparently emanating from a 'Northern Theory' background (Connell, 2007). It also placed them within Rogoff's (2003) sociocultural orienting concepts as they examined, reflected and re-examined the notion that there is no 'one best way' to approach learning and teaching (2003: 12). The building of relationships of trust, and the recognition and articulation of power deriving from the external positioning of the Australian researchers as 'experts' by the project initiators and funders prefaced the importance to Christine and Linda of respecting project participants as knowers: competent and capable agents in their own context. Silvia, in reflecting on her own increasing participation and agency in the project, says that action research allowed practitioners to broaden their perspective. Everything became associated to their daily routine and as such provided resources to generate new research as new topics to tackle came up. Silvia says:

> The deep theory and strategy knowledge the Australian researchers have, plus the practitioner's management of the local reality, is an ideal complement and has allowed taking up any research and/or new themes to study. As new knowledge and new ideas to research were captured and generated in conjunction, the programme became sustainable.

The extensive resources of practitioner action research provided a solid framework for identifying and articulating an approach strongly underpinned by an ethics of relationship (Groundwater-Smith and Mockler, 2008; Mockler, 2014; Semetsky, 2012). This secured the place of commitments to collaboration in knowledge construction, capacity building and visibility in negotiating relationships. Christine and Linda were committed to learning thorough 'insider/outsider' communication which needed to 'include the perspectives of other communities [where] it is not a matter of which perspective is correct as both have an angle on the phenomena that helps to build understanding' (Rogoff, 2003: 24).

Silvia and Mónica, reflecting on active participation as co-researchers, note that it meant many things. Mónica says:

> It also means to me that I and my team must be prepared and keep the FIH methodology implementation renewed, adding elements for continuous improvement. The Australian team gave me the opportunity to realise those things and through the people who are close to me, family and community, things I couldn't do in the classroom I now can. I feel lucky to have this team. It is the best labour atmosphere. I have grown much as a professional. This project has allowed me to transmit to the others through different ways, the essence of the project. In the beginning it was difficult for me to understand but once I got it I made it mine. I think it has given good results. I am competitive in a good way.

Findings

Two levels of data analysis are now discussed. In the first level of analysis, photostories and accompanying descriptive scripts were examined. In the second, the reflective account is discussed. A great deal of change is clearly evident for both Silvia and Mónica.

Photostory analysis

Mónica's photostories focused on her leadership of classroom change. Each of the 'before' descriptions of educators in one of her rooms fell into the historical category, with two in individual, and one in interpersonal. Mónica described an individual, rather than interpersonal situation where, before the project:

> The adult doesn't provide a visual interaction; adults don't interact at children's height so it doesn't produce wanted interest [from children]; the adult's attitude doesn't allow interactions.

Examination of one 'before' photograph (Figure 2.1) reveals at least 40 per cent (four of ten) of the children shown are actively looking away from the educator who is fully absorbed in her own personal teaching delivery.

Figure 2.1 also shows that Mónica's 'after' descriptions show a clear shift and fall evenly across the three planes of analysis (individual,

RELATO FOTOGRÁFICO

El Jardín Fundación Minera Escondida se encuentra inserto en el sector norte alto de la ciudad de Antofagasta. Posee una infraestructura moderna y una implementación que seduce e invita a las familias a ser usuarias de él. Atiende a 136 niñas y niños desde 3 meses a 3 años 11 meses. El equipo de trabajo está compuesto por 6 educadoras de párvulos, 11 técnicas en atención de párvulos, 2 auxiliares de servicio, 1 administrativa. El nivel socioeconómico del lugar es bajo, producto de trabajos ocasionales de las familias que lo componen. Además, existe gran vulnerabilidad social y alto riesgo por el tráfico y consumo de drogas que afecta el sector.

Las familias usuarias del establecimiento, una vez que sus hijas e hijos comienzan a asistir al jardín, comienzan a involucrarse en el proceso educativo de sus hijas e hijos trabajando paralelamente con el jardín infantil.

En relación al proyecto piloto Futuro Infantil Hoy, el equipo de educadoras y técnicas, desarrollaba un trabajo relevante y significativo para las niñas y niños y sus familias, sin embargo, buscando nuevas metodologías para innovar, aceptamos el desafío con mucho agrado y entusiasmo, reformulando y potenciando las prácticas pedagógicas, insertando nuevas estratégicas metodológicas , las que en forma paulatina, mediante talleres y mesas redondas de liderazgo, fueron enriqueciendo el quehacer educativo.

Antes

El adulto no propicia una interacción visual.	Los adultos no interactúan a la altura de las niñas y niños no se produce el interés deseado.	La actitud de los adultos no favorece las Interacciones.

Este proyecto aportó nuevos conceptos, los que fueron incorporados en la práctica diaria en todos los niveles de atención. Uno de los más relevantes es el de literacidad, aplicable en el jardín , hogar y comunidad. La priorización de actividades en pequeños grupos, ha permitido que sea mas personalizada la entrega de aprendizajes con interacciones espontáneas e inmediatas, el desarrollo del pensamiento sostenido compartido, la co-construcción adulto niño, niño-niño, se incorporaron con grandes resultados. La implementación de las salas y patios está de acuerdo a los intereses y propuestas de las y sus familias y los elementos de éstas, a su altura e inmediato alcance. Se ha adquirido la metodología de mostrar, especialmente a las familias, la forma secuencial del desarrollo de las actividades, mediante fotografías, se han implementado obras de arte creadas por las niñas y niños, lo que forma parte de la ornamentación de las salas

También, se ha implementado la autolectura potenciando la creatividad, el conocimiento del entorno, la convivencia, la identidad, el razonamiento lógico y la reflexión.

Respecto a la familia, se ha incrementado considerablemente la participación con sus aportes desde sus espacios, transformando vivencias e historias de vida en portafolios y libros, lo que hace más cercana su relación con las educadoras y técnicas y por lo tanto, se involucran, con mayor interés en el proceso educativo de sus hijas e hijos, además, aportar sus fondos de conocimientos enriquecen sus aprendizajes , lo que las hace sentir valoradas como personas y primeras educadoras y protagonistas de la educación de ellos.

Este proyecto piloto conciliado con nuestra formación profesional y con nuestro referente curricular institucional, potenció al **Jardín Fundación Minera Escondida**, reconocido por nuestros directivos, pares, comunidad y especialmente, por las familias como un gran **Centro de Aprendizajes para las niñas y niños preescolares,** y al haber sido capaz de internalizar la esencia de éste proyecto, nuestro equipo dice **Futuro Infantil ahora y siempre.**

DESPUÉS

Los niños y niñas proponen y deciden.	Los adultos interactúan a la altura de las niñas y niños y se produce el interés deseado.	La posición del adulto permite un aprendizaje mediado.

Figure 2.1 Mónica's photostory (relato fotográfico)

interpersonal and community/institutional change) but are all in the cultural issues category.

Children propose and decide [ideas and interests]; family sharing their funds of knowledge; adult's position allows mediated learning. Figure 2.1 shows the dramatic change in one educator's positioning and pedagogical approach. All children in the 'after' photograph appear fully engaged in co-constructing learning with the educator, demonstrating a clear shift in the educator's pedagogical approach towards a socioculturally responsive repositioning, reflected by Mónica when she further discusses the sustainability of the new sociocultural approaches elsewhere in the chapter.

RELATO FOTOGRÁFICO

Presentación del proyecto por parte de la Universidad de Western Sydney.

Inicio del Proyecto

Año 2009 se cambia la mirada y se comienza a dar espacios de participación a las agentes educativas como personas que tienen mucho que aportar y que pueden liderar.

Fines del año 2009 inicio año 2010 estrategias que potencian la integración de la familia siendo estas valoradas y participando activamente en el proceso pedagógico.

Se da importancia a la cultura de cada niño y de su familia, se integra a los ambientes elementos de otros países. 2009-2010

Se crearon durante el año 2009 y 2010 proyectos en base a los intereses de los niños que lograron la integración y participación de la familia y de todo el jardín, liderando estos procesos la agente educativa

Estrategias como los portafolios permitieron el cambio de concepto que los padres tenían en relación a la función del jardín infantil pasando de ser un centro solamente asistencia a ser un centro pedagógico de apoyo a la familia.

Figure 2.2 Silvia's photostory

Silvia's 'before' descriptions were primarily clustered in the individual/cultural category (three descriptions), with one in the institutional change/cultural category. Early change is already described for children, families and educators. Her photos and descriptors focus on early stages of the project, when she was a centre director, and imply the shift from previous practice, rather than explicitly describing it:

> In 2009 changes include that educational assistants started having participation spaces, are [newly] seen as people with lots to contribute, and have leading capacities [and at the] end of 2009 into 2010, strategies boost family participation. Families are valued and are [now] actively involved in the pedagogical process.

Her 'after' descriptions all fall within the cultural issues category, with the majority (seven of eleven units of meaning) being in the community/institutional change category. There are two units of meaning in each of the individual and interpersonal categories:

> Children and family cultural backgrounds are [now] acknowledged, learning environments [now] include elements from other countries [of family origin]; projects based in children's interests are [now] implemented, achieving family and staff centre integration and participation, all [newly] lead by the educational assistants; strategies like the [pedagogical documentation] portfolios changed the concept parents had of the centre being just an assistance centre, to be seen as a pedagogical centre that supports the family.

Analysis of photostory reflective account

A simple tally count of units of meaning, shown in Table 2.2, reveals that the majority of units in all 'after' photostories fall within the community/institutional change/cultural category of the analysis matrix. When considering the sociocultural variables of historical, cultural and contextual, it can be seen that the cultural variable drew the most thought and comment from Silvia and Mónica. Within the three planes of analysis (individual, interpersonal and community/institution), most were related to community/institutional, indicating a shift and commitment on Silvia and Mónica's part to sociocultural approaches.

In her explanation Mónica reflects how the centre team have incorporated the socioculturally informed concepts learned during the successive cycles of practitioner research. She reveals a shift from her former focus on the historical and the individual towards a strong focus on intra-personal and cultural elements of her work.

Table 2.2   Unit of meaning tally

	Historical issues	Cultural issues	Contextual issues	Total
Individual	5	15	4	29
Interpersonal	1	15	2	19
Community/institutional change	3	26	9	28
Total	9	56	15	

Reformulating and strengthening pedagogical practices, inserting new strategies and methodologies gradually enriched our educational routine. FIH provided new concepts which were incorporated in all the levels of the centre's daily practice. The prioritisation of activities in small groups allowed for a more personalised learning delivery process, spontaneous and immediate interactions, sustained shared thinking development, co-construction, child–child and adult–child, were incorporated with great results. Children and their family's interests and suggestions were incorporated. … We have acquired methodologies of display, especially to show families the sequence of development of activities and children's art-work is part of classroom display. … In relation to the family, its participation increased considerably, contributing from their homes and communities, transforming life stories and experiences into portfolios and books. As a consequence the relationship between educators and families became a lot closer; parents were more interested in becoming engaged in their children's educational process. They also brought their funds of knowledge, enriching children's learning. They felt valued as individuals and first educators of their children. After the pilot, our educational team has experienced an important change in the way they deliver learning, the way they listen to children, giving them more space, listening to their ideas and providing children with a main role in their routine.

Conclusions and insights gained

Data analysis and subsequent conversations have illuminated important issues associated with engaging in collaborative activities in which a curriculum and pedagogical change agenda is foregrounded.

(Continued)

(Continued)

Our shared investigation of the research questions has revealed a robust and encouraging indication that Silvia and Mónica as practitioner researchers have definitely found socioculturally informed approaches to be achievable, useful and beneficial for interpersonal and community pedagogical leadership. Importantly, sociocultural approaches, locally adapted in a Chilean context in communities of extreme poverty, are accessible, understandable and can be used to successfully engage Chilean educators in processes of family engagement. Silvia and Mónica's teams of Chilean practitioner researchers were willing and ready to take up resources introduced by Australian researchers and apply them in unique and culturally relevant ways. Challenges in reforming practices are similar to those in other places. They involve time, varying levels of support, resistances to change, deep reflection on professional identity, and challenges to current ways of being. Overall, however, we all agree that challenges are far outweighed by the benefits.

Analysis of the co-constructed data in this chapter has demonstrated the strengths of the sociocultural approach and research framework that evolved. Silvia and Mónica have shown clear evidence of a professional growth that would have been unlikely prior to this project, or within a prescribed 'top-down' short-term professional development programme. Linda and Christine have both been through an enormous professional learning curve as they have planned, negotiated, co-constructed, learnt, worked across cultures, suggested research approaches and devised socioculturally relevant data generation and analysis methods.

There is evidence, mainly from Mónica, that the project and collaborative research has strengthened knowledge, awareness and practice in the area of socioculturally informed mediating strategies with children such as scaffolding, and in community change with families, indicating a shift towards 'integrating children's voices and views' and ensuring that they are recognised as social actors and no longer invisible, as advocated by Galdames (2011: 119). She believes that for her FIH is now sustainable with all daily planning including FIH concepts. Monica said:

Children have to be active, creative etc. so 'he/she is a child of FIH'. The questions of the Australian team shifted my thinking. We have combined the Basis [Chilean curriculum] with FIH. Professional learning has been built into daily processes so FIH is now sustainable. The pilot finished in 2010. It finished there because the date finished there but we have not finished. This centre is live proof that the programme is sustainable. We are always changing and the children and families are always interested.

Another encouraging shift indicated primarily by Silvia is a greatly increased level of professional agency evident in the work of *technicas*, who prior to the project, were largely restrained to the technical work of preparing materials, moving furniture and cleaning up. This encouragingly demonstrates what Galdames has called 'a potential space of agency', which has been achieved through our shared 'research and educational practice, analytical deconstruction and reconstruction' of the status quo in centres (2011: 119).

A third change discussed by both Silvia and Mónica involves a repositioning of children and families to now recognise their historical relationships. Individual children and family members are now recognised as having backgrounds and strengths worth finding out about, allowing educators to meaningfully bring their cultural realities into classroom practice. Children are newly acknowledged 'as social actors' who are citizens and 'highly knowledgeable about their lives and context' (Galdames, 2011: 119).

These issues are centrally important in building deeper understandings about factors implicated in mobilising pedagogical change, and the significant ways sociocultural approaches might contribute to improving quality of children's learning, enhancing family involvement and addressing inequalities deriving from children's experience of living in social disadvantage.

Closing thoughts

Silvia and Mónica have shown through their recorded narratives and reflections that their thinking and practice has shifted from a more personal-individual and historical way of being to a socioculturally informed identity where their thinking and practice shows greater strength in the interpersonal and community change areas, reflecting cultural contextual awareness.

Mónica sees it as a privilege to have professional associations that complement her leadership role. She explains that before FIH her working community was not recognised or visible as a successful centre and they were not valued in the way they wanted. When FIH started, the centre began to be recognised for the implementation of innovative methodologies and now they are recognised as the best centre in the region.

Silvia thinks the benefits are clearly to do with children's learning improvement and family integration but that overall educational teams need to see things differently, from a new insight, a *cambiar la mirada* (change of vision) when doing their practice. She advocates that educators must believe in their project and dare to implement changes in early childhood education.

Ongoing research considerations

For ourselves, and other researchers we offer the following provocations for consideration:

- How can the processes of practitioner research be used, or used differently in your work?
- What changes could be made in your work that could draw on the practitioner research approach?
- And finally, in order to undertake achievable and successful research, think of a small team with whom you would like to work in a practitioner research project.

References

Alexander, R. (2001) 'Border crossings: towards a comparative pedagogy', *Comparative Education*, 37 (4): 507–23.

Alvesson, M. and Sköldberg, K. (2009) *Reflexive Methodology. New Vistas for Qualitative Research*. London: Sage.

Antofagasta (n.d.) Retrieved from Wikipedia, http://en.wikipedia.org/wiki/Antofagasta (last accessed 9 December 2014).

Ashton, J. and Newman, L. (2006) 'An unfinished symphony: 21st century teacher education using knowledge creating Heutagogies', *British Journal of Educational Technology*, 37 (6): 837–52.

Cochran-Smith, M. and Lytle, S. (2007) 'Everything's ethics: practitioner inquiry and university culture', in A. Campbell and S. Groundwater-Smith (eds), *An Ethical Approach to Practitioner Research: Dealing with Issues*. Hokoben, NY: Routledge, pp. 24–41.

Cohen, L., Manion, L. and Morrison, K. (2007) *Research Methods in Education* (6th edn). London: Routledge.

Connell, R. (2007) 'The northern theory of globalization', *Sociological Theory*, 25 (4): 368–85.

Denzin, N. K. and Lincoln, Y. S. (2013) *The Landscape of Qualitative Research* (4th edn). Thousand Oaks, CA: Sage.

Edwards, S. (2006) '"Stop thinking of culture as geography": early childhood educators' conceptions of sociocultural theory as an informant to curriculum', *Contemporary Issues in Early Childhood*, 7 (3): 238–52.

Fleer, M. (2014) 'Beyond developmental geology: a cultural-historical theorization of digital visual technologies for studying young children's development', in M. Fleer and A. Ridgway (eds), *Visual Methodologies and Digital Tools for Researching with Young Children: Transforming Visuality*. Switzerland: Springer, pp. 15–34.

Galdames, P. (2011) 'Chilean early childhood education as a promoter of social justice: challenging neo-colonial trajectories of knowledge', *International Studies in Education*, 12: 106–24.

Gonzalez, N., Moll, L. and Amanti, C. (2005) *Funds of Knowledge. Theorizing Practices in Households, Communities and Classrooms*. New Jersey: Lawrence Erlbaum Associates Inc.

Gray, C. and MacBlain, S. (2012) *Learning Theories in Childhood*. London: Sage.

Groundwater-Smith, S. and Mockler, N. (2008) 'Ethics in practitioner research: an issue of quality', in J. Furlong and A. Oancea (eds), *Assessing Quality in Applied Practice Based Educational Research*. Oxford: Oxford University Department of Educational Studies, pp. 80–91.

Mockler, N. (2014) 'When "research ethics" become "everyday ethics": the intersection of inquiry and practice in practitioner research', *Educational Action Research*, 22 (2): 146–58.

Moje, E., Ciechanowski, K., Kramer, K., Ellis, L., Carillo, R. and Cillazo, T. (2004) 'Working toward third space in content area literacy: an examination of everyday funds of knowledge and discourse', *Reading Research Quarterly*, 39 (1): 38–49.

Newman, L. and Ashton, J. (2009) 'Sociocultural learning approaches: exploring early childhood communities of practice', *Australian Research in Early Childhood Education*, 16 (1): 87–101.

Newman, L. and Woodrow, C. (2007) 'Moving beyond "prac": building communities of practice', *Every Child*, 13 (1): 14–15.

Newman, L., Woodrow, C. and Arthur, L. (2014) 'Visible difference: photostory as an evaluation and capacity building method'. Manuscript submitted for publication.

Parra, C. and Franks, D. (2011) 'Monitoring social progress in mining zones – the case of Antofagasta and Tarapacá, Chile', *SR Mining* 2011, First National Seminar in Social Responsibility in Mining, 19–21 October 2011, Santiago Chile.

Pennington, J., Brock, C., Palmer, T. and Wolters, L. (2013) 'Opportunities to teach: confronting the deskilling of teachers through the development of teacher knowledge of multiple literacies', *Teachers and Teaching: Theory and Practice*, 19 (1): 63–77.

Perry, K. (2012) 'What is literacy? A critical overview of sociocultural perspectives', *Journal of Language and Literacy Education*, 8 (1): 51–71.

Pink, S. (2005) *The Future of Visual Ethnography: Engaging the Senses*. Abingdon: Routledge.

Pink, S. (2013) *Doing Visual Ethnography* (3rd edn). London: Sage.

Rogoff, B. (1998) 'Cognition as a collaborative process', in D. Kuhn and R. S. Siegler (eds), *Cognition, Perception and Language*, Vol. 2, *Handbook of Child Psychology* (5th edn), ed. W. Damon. New York: Wiley, pp. 679–744.

Rogoff, B. (2003) *The Cultural Nature of Human Development*. New York: Oxford University Press.

Rogoff, B. (n.d.) 'Observing sociocultural activity on three planes: participatory appropriation, guided participation, and apprenticeship'. Retrieved from: http://people.ucsc.edu/~gwells/Files/Courses_Folder/documents/Rogoff. Part-Appr.pdf (last accessed 22 May 2015).

Rose, G. (2007) *Visual Methodologies: An Introduction to the Interpretation of Visual Materials* (2nd edn). London: Sage.

Semetsky, I. (2012) 'Living, learning, loving: constructing a new ethics of integration in education', *Discourse: Studies in the Cultural Politics of Education*, 33 (1): 47–59.

Umayahara, M. (2006) 'Early childhood education policies in Chile: from pre-Jomtien to post-Dakar', background paper prepared for the *Education for All Global Monitoring Report 2007. Strong Foundations: Early Childhood Care and Education*. United Nations Educational, Scientific and Cultural Organization. Retrieved from: www.researchconnections.org/childcare/resources/11837 (last accessed 8 December 2014).

Veresov, N. (2014) 'Method, methodology and methodological thinking', in M. Fleer and A. Ridgway (eds), *Visual Methodologies and Digital Tools for Researching with Young Children: Transforming Visuality*. Switzerland: Springer, pp. 215–28.

Vygotsky, L. S. (1978) *Mind in Society: The Development of Higher Psychological Processes*. Cambridge, MA: Harvard University Press.

Woodrow, C., Arthur, L. and Newman, L. (2014) 'Community capacity building: perspectives on international early childhood literacy development in Futuro Infantil Hoy', in L. Arthur, J. Ashton and B. Beecher (eds), *Diverse Literacies and Social Justice: Implications for Practice*. Melbourne: Australian Council for Educational Research, pp. 86–105.

3

INSIDER ISLAMIC SPACES OF INQUIRY: MUSLIM EDUCATORS PRODUCING NEW KNOWLEDGE IN SYDNEY, AUSTRALIA

Oznur Aydemir, Fatima Mourad, Leonie Arthur and Jen Skattebol

Key words   epistemic disobedience; intercultural dialogue; collaborative practitioner research; knowledge production.

Chapter overview

In this chapter we share the challenges of educators working 'against the grain' (de Castell, 1993: 185) of orthodox knowledge and explore the enabling contribution of what we have termed 'insider Islamic spaces of inquiry' to generate new knowledge. The chapter draws on data from a practitioner research project involving a group of Muslim teachers working in Muslim schools and secular early childhood settings in Sydney, Australia. This was one of three groups nested in a larger project, named the Collaborative Practitioner Research Project (Skattebol and Arthur, 2014). The members of this group of Muslim practitioners named themselves the *Habibties*, which loosely means friends/darlings/honeys in Arabic and is used to show affection and friendship. This chapter discusses three research projects – Oznur's research on music teaching in Islamic schools, Fatima's research on the professional identities of Muslim educators in a secular setting,

(Continued)

(Continued)

and Jen and Leonie's research on the processes of practitioner research. The key themes addressed in the chapter are collaborative practitioner research as a space for critical reflection; combining practitioner research with post-colonial theory to open up possibilities for practitioners to produce their own culturally relevant knowledge; and insider spaces of inquiry as particularly important for marginalised groups navigating cultural interfaces as they work across boundaries (Manathunga, 2009). Readers can expect to learn about findings from a project that provided insights into the broader dynamics of collaborative practitioner research practice as well as themes particular to Islamic educational contexts. The chapter provides evidence of the role of collaborative practitioner research as an important avenue for the production of a democratic palette of knowledge to inform teaching.

How the authors came to be working together

A safe space is necessary if practitioners are to challenge dominant discourses and engage in productive dialogue across the cultural interface. The idea of an insider Islamic space for inquiry was co-constructed over several informal conversations between the four authors. It was initiated by one of the authors, Oznur Aydemir, who used her existing networks to invite potential practitioner researchers to join the group and hosted an introductory meeting with the practitioners and the academic partners in her home, where a group of practitioner researchers, called the *Habibties*, was formed.

Oznur is a teacher in Islamic schools and is interested in destabilising the static and limiting constructions of Muslims embedded in Orientalist discourses. She has a continuing interest in exploring the inclusion of religion, or more broadly spirituality, in teacher education programmes to promote better understanding of how this may influence teaching and learning in schools.

Another key member of the *Habibties* group was Fatima Mourad, who is the director of a secular early childhood centre and interested in the potential of practitioner research to develop leadership capacity. Fatima works to integrate Islamic knowledge at all levels of educational practice and theory. To this end she is a strong advocate for greater representation of Muslim voices and hopes to foreground Muslim identities, social, cultural and linguistic knowledge in education. She believes current policies need to be revisioned if the issues facing marginalised communities are to be effectively addressed.

The two university-based academics, Jen Skattebol and Leonie Arthur, played the role of critical friends to the three concurrent practitioner research groups and researched the processes of practitioner research. Jen and Leonie are Anglo-Australians who taught in a teacher education programme from which Oznur and Fatima had graduated. This course had a strong focus on diversity and culturally responsive learning environments and used post-structural theory to elucidate power relations in educational settings. Jen and Leonie were committed to developing 'intercultural dialogues' (Manathunga, 2009) that can facilitate greater understanding in the academy. As teaching academics they were committed to providing opportunities for educators to produce their own contextually relevant knowledge and pedagogies and interested in researching the processes of collaborative practitioner research.

Rationale for the study

Australia's Muslim population has increased rapidly, growing by 69 per cent between 2001 and 2011 to a total of 2.2 per cent of the population (Australian Bureau of Statistics, 2012). There has been a concomitant expansion of the Islamic school sector, with current figures showing 35 across Australia and 19 in our state of New South Wales (Hassen, 2013), which is similar to trends in other Western countries (Memon, 2011). Despite this growth in Islamic schools, and in the number of Muslim teachers graduating from universities, little is known about the career trajectories of these teachers or about how they negotiate their everyday practices and professional identities once they are in the workforce. The Australian teaching profession is predominantly monolingual and Anglo-Celtic (McKenzie et al., 2008). The nuances of working in Islamic schools or as a Muslim practitioner in secular early childhood settings are generally not systematically or rigorously addressed in initial teacher education programmes. In addition, there is little research on the principles of Islamic pedagogy or how it may be valued or included in Western teacher education courses (Memon, 2011).

Since 2001 Muslims and Islamic religious beliefs, values and practices have been the focus of attention 'fomented by divisive discourses' emanating from politicians and the media (Halafoff, 2011: 455) and have been viewed by many as a global threat (Saeed, 2003). The resultant 'Islamophobia' (Poynting and Mason, 2007) has generated discrimination against Muslims and an increase in practices which demean and exclude them from economic, social and public life (Gottschalk and Greenberg, 2007), exacerbating their fear of scrutiny and resulting in isolation. As a result, Islamic schools and early childhood services tend to be isolated and operate as an enclave and, as Zine (2006) argues, tend to insulate students from the outside world.

More needs to be known about what Australian Islamic schools and early childhood services look like, and the daily experiences of Muslim educators in the Islamic and secular education sectors. We need to know whether there is dissonance between the values embedded in Australian teacher education programmes and the expectations of Islamic educational settings, families and communities and how value dissonances are negotiated in everyday practices. There is also a need for greater understanding about the diversity of Islamic thought and how this informs responsive teaching practices for the array of Muslim communities.

Zembylas (2004: 936) has argued that all professional identities can be considered to be 'contingent and fragile, and thus open for reconstruction'. The *Habibties* were interested in finding out how professional identities were constructed and reconstructed by Muslim educators working across Muslim and secular educational institutions under the pressures of Islamophobia. Given that professional identities are shaped by 'social and structural relations' (Dillabough, 1999: 22), Muslim educators are likely to be influenced by the different discourses available to them, including those about what it is to be a 'good educator' and a 'good Muslim' within the context of Islamophobia.

Aims

The overarching aim of the Collaborative Practitioner Research Project was to provide an environment where educators could identify and research their own dilemmas, produce their own knowledge, explore their professional identities and enhance their leadership skills. It also aimed to facilitate critical dialogue between the academy and the field of practice and between Muslim and non-Muslim educators.

As academics and practitioners we were politically committed to research that resists the pressure to speak with one voice. We were interested in generating multiple perspectives about teaching, academia, the early childhood field, being a Muslim educator and so on. We hoped the multiplicity of these perspectives could challenge universalist assumptions that there is a 'good' teacher/a 'good' Muslim. In this we found it necessary to acknowledge the dominant power relations between the academy and the field and between Muslims and non-Muslims and to be reflexive in our approach to these fields of power. We aimed to generate practitioner stories that allowed 'unassimilated otherness' (Young, 2011: 227). The collaborative approach to practitioner research aimed to provide the emotional and intellectual support that facilitates educators' reflection, critique and action (Goodfellow and Hedges, 2006).

Theoretical perspectives

Collaborative practitioner research is a methodology that enables educators to research their own issues and dilemmas and produce their own contextually relevant knowledges, and as such was ideally suited to the *Habibties'* inquiries. The term collaborative practitioner research reflects the critical role of communities of learners in facilitating professional dialogue, critical reflection and critical action (Skattebol and Arthur, 2014). This methodology has the potential to break down the traditional dichotomy and the uneven power relationships between the academy and the field and between Muslim and non-Muslim educators to create a third space (Bhabha, 1994) for the production of new contextually relevant knowledge.

Post-colonial theory offers important conceptual frameworks to inform equity driven practitioner research practices. It opens up spaces that enable the contestation of dominant discourses of early childhood education and the academic/practitioner and Muslim/non-Muslim dichotomies. Post-colonial perspectives recognise and value 'knowledges developed outside the dominant hegemonic orientation of the West' (Rizvi, 2004: 161) and allow for 'epistemic disobedience' (Mignolo, 2009: 160) that challenges the Western assumption that there is one way to interpret the world. As Nakata et al. (2012) argue, post-colonial theory challenges the idealising and universalising of Western thought and allows for 'epistemic awakening' (Wiredu, 1995) and 'decolonial knowledge-making' (Nakata et al., 2012: 124).

We draw on Said's (1994) view of educational institutions as sites of both colonial power and post-colonial aspiration in order to reconceptualise possible relations between academic researchers and teacher practitioners and between Muslim and non-Muslim educators. We are interested in how the post-colonial notion of the 'contact zone' (Pratt, 1992: 4) contributes to productive cross-cultural exchanges and knowledge creation (Manathunga, 2009: 165) across Muslim/non-Muslim and academic/practitioner contexts. This 'cultural space' (Pratt, 1992: 4) provides a space for cultural exchange through 'copresence, interaction, interlocking understandings and practices' (1992: 7).

Traditionally the academy holds the epistemological power to define and delimit educational practices and subjects (Rizvi and Lingard, 2006). This power, however, is also undone and troubled through strategic alliances that refigure the relations between the 'centre' (that is the academy) and its margins (in this case the early childhood field and more specifically Muslim educators).

Collaborative practitioner research

As indicated earlier in this chapter the *Habibties* ran concurrently with two other groups under an umbrella Collaborative Practitioner Research Project that aimed to generate process knowledge about practitioner research. The *Habibties* followed the same broad action research processes as the other groups.

Each distinct group met with the university-based critical friends monthly to share dilemmas, engage in reflexive inquiry in communities of practice and discuss their research projects. Practitioners discussed current practices in their settings; shared and deconstructed dilemma stories (Whalley et al., 2004); identified common threads, underlying values and principles; and planned actions.

Processes used within the collaborative practitioner research groups provided a scaffold that enabled each educator to identify a broad research interest and then develop and refine a clear, manageable research question. Educators pursued questions that were significant to them and relevant to their local context. Once they had mapped existing knowledge, these practitioner researchers developed an ethical framework for action, decided on methods of data collection, and then collected their data. At subsequent meetings they shared excerpts of this data with the group and engaged in joint analysis. The ethics of collaborative practitioner research, including the importance of open communication, attentive listening, mutual respect, democratic processes and trust (Whalley et al., 2004) was emphasised and modelled by the academic partners throughout the project. The university academics were positioned as critical friends, rather than the holders of knowledge, and practitioners as the experts and knowledge producers (Dimitriadis, 2006).

Description of studies

Three discrete studies are reported in this chapter. The first is Fatima's research into Muslim educators' professional identities, the second is Oznur's research about teaching music in Muslim schools and the last is Leonie and Jen's research about collaborative practitioner research processes.

Muslim educators' professional identities

Fatima's overarching question for her practitioner research was: How do Muslim educators' identities impact on their professionalism in secular early childhood settings within the context of global troubles? This question responded to anecdotal evidence that Muslim educators felt that they had been compelled to silence their Islamic knowledge and beliefs in their professional practice with children and families within secular early childhood services. Fatima was interested in investigating how the context of global events such as the September 11 attacks on the World Trade Center in New York (2001), the 2002 Bali bombings, and local events such as the 2005 Cronulla Riots[1] in Sydney, impacted on educators' perceptions of self within their workplace and how conscious they had become of their Muslim identity. The research project as a whole aimed to develop conceptual frameworks and identify implications for service delivery for promoting social inclusion and a sense of security for children, families and educators.

Islamic epistemologies and Western music curriculum

Oznur's research question focused on how teachers negotiate state-mandated curriculum while simultaneously implementing music programmes that also embrace Islamic beliefs, culture and pedagogies. The research aimed to investigate and invigorate ways in which Muslim primary teachers can expand their teaching of music, using music that is relevant to the Muslim context and that draws on teachers' personal experiences, interests and capabilities.

The Collaborative Practitioner Research Project

The research conducted by Leonie and Jen focused on the role of practitioner research in building transformative leadership and curriculum change. It investigated the complexities of academic/field partnerships in collaborative practitioner research.

---

[1]On 11 December 2005 a riot occurred on Cronulla Beach in Sydney targeting men of 'Middle Eastern appearance'. Many Lebanese-Australians retaliated in response to Anglo-Australian racial taunts and messages promoting 'Aussie Pride'. Social media as well as local radio played a key role in mobilising the rioters and those who retaliated. See www.sbs.com.au/cronullariots/ (last accessed 24 February 2015).

Methodology

While the educators were inducted into action research processes and their role as practitioner researchers, each project took on its own life and methodology. However, all projects were dynamic, positioned as action research and used qualitative approaches to data collection.

Data collection

Fatima's research into Muslim educators' professional identities was undertaken in two early childhood settings situated in south west Sydney, where the majority of the population is low socio-economic, Christian and Anglo-Australian, with around 1.5 per cent Muslims. Early Childhood Setting 1 enrolled children predominantly from Christian, Anglo-Australian families while Early Childhood Setting 2 had a larger number of Muslims in the local community and in the centre.

Phase one of the research involved interviews that explored educators' views about their professional identities. Seven Muslim staff, including Muslim Lebanese, Muslim Iraqis and Muslim Indian-Afghan educators with a range of qualifications and experiences from each of the settings participated in semi-structured interviews of approximately 30 minutes. These interviews were conducted by Fatima herself in one setting and by the owner of the two centres (also a Muslim) at the other setting. Fatima also engaged in ongoing dialogue and reflective conversations with educators about their professional identities based on early findings.

Oznur's research about Islamic epistemologies and Western music curriculum involved six teachers teaching across Kindergarten to Year 6 in a Muslim primary school where she was the leader of the creative arts programme. In Stage 1 of the action research cycle Oznur conducted informal interviews with teachers and collected artefacts such as music related lesson plans. In Stage 2, in her role as creative arts coordinator, she offered and presented three professional learning music workshops based on her analysis of the data collected in Stage 1 interviews. Stage 3 involved the collection of artefacts generated after changes were made.

Jen and Leonie's research involved conducting a cycle of interviews and/or focus groups at the beginning and conclusion of the project with practitioners, and the academics who were critical friends.

Challenges

Each of the distinct groups experienced similar challenges. All the practitioner research groups including the *Habibties* faced an absence of
institutional support for either or both the practitioner research initiative
and knowledge production. No release time was provided for educators,
meaning they had to sustain their research in their own time. There were
also no habits of transparency and peer review in the schools and centres, and therefore there were few opportunities for educators to bring
private, individual work or workplace dilemmas into the public domain.
Practitioners were uncertain, and to a certain extent fearful, about opening their practices to scrutiny and they needed time to build relationships
and to find a language to engage in critique of their practices. This fear
of outside scrutiny was amplified in the *Habibties* group where the risks
of epistemic disobedience were highest. Epistemic disobedience means
'delinking' (Mignolo, 2009: 160) from Western and colonial ideas and
ideals that position some regions and people as 'underdeveloped economically and mentally' (Mignolo, 2009: 161). One of the risks facing the
Habibties was that the academic researchers would not understand the
complexities of the dilemmas they faced nor the risks that they were taking
in engaging in practitioner research, leaving them vulnerable and exposed.

Discussion of findings

The findings reported here emanate both from Fatima's and Oznur's individual practitioner research projects and the overarching research into
collaborative practitioner research conducted by Jen and Leonie. Each of
these is reported below.

The impact of Islamophobia on Muslim educators' professional identities

Analysis of the interview data revealed that Islamophobia had a direct
impact on the Muslim educators who participated in Fatima's study, illus-
trating how participating Muslim educators foregrounded or backgrounded
aspects of Islamic practice and beliefs depending on who they were
interacting with and in which context. Like the Muslim girls in Zine's
(2006: 247) Canadian study, educators 'script[ed] their identities by resisting or accommodating themselves' to a range of competing constructions.

It was evident that most participants within Fatima's study had become more conscious of risks posed by their Muslim identities since major events such as the September 11 attacks. The data showed that there was a heightened sense of fear about non-Muslims' perceptions of Muslim educators that was fuelled by the negative media coverage. Educators in both the Muslim dominated and secular setting stated that they felt the need to prove they are 'good Muslims' so that negative stereotypical discourses are challenged.

The educators felt that they had been largely stereotyped as 'terrorists' and 'backwards' within the media, and this impacted on the way families within their secular workplace interacted with them. In this situation of heightened Islamophobia, the Muslim educators explained that they had to constantly defend their Islamic beliefs and explain how their practices do not support acts of terrorism. Global events such as September 11 and the local Cronulla riots resulted in educators feeling that they were treated as suspects by some non-Muslims. As Rivzi (2004: 162) argues, September 11 produced a 'powerful new narrative of security ... that rendered the relationship between the West and Islam into one of antagonism', the global effects of which were experienced locally. Negative media coverage made some educators conscious that they are perceived as 'barbaric and cannot be trusted'. One educator commented:

> I have fears with non-Muslim families since September 11. In terms of working with non-Muslims I'm always afraid they will look at me differently because of negative media coverage. I feel that media impacts on how families view me and the way they see me working with children.

Negative media commentary attesting to the role of Islamic schools exacerbating cultural divisions in society (Buckingham, 2010) fuelled these Muslim educators' sense of being 'suspect'. When one of the early childhood settings employed more Muslim staff, educators reported that some non-Muslim parents expressed concerns that 'Muslim workers have taken over'.

Furthermore, the Muslim educators in this study felt positioned as disempowered as women. Zine (2006) describes a nexus of 'gendered Islamophobia' (Zine, 2006: 240) that resonates with the complexities articulated by the practitioners. This nexus is the centre of discourses which posit Muslim women as oppressed and in need of emancipation on one axis and an array of expectations of what it is to be a 'good Muslim' from Muslim communities on the other axis. The practitioners described this as they discussed moving in and out of asserting and practising their Muslim identity – wearing and removing the *hijab* (headscarf) strategically in response to fears of discrimination and loss of job opportunities in secular workplaces and/or their desires to fit the image of 'good' Muslim women in the Muslim community.

Their Muslim identities were expressed strategically. One Muslim practitioner chose to wear a hat in the secular early childhood setting instead of the *hijab* so that her 'Muslim identity' was not obvious through her dress code. As Zine (2006: 242) notes, the veil has become a marker of otherness and a 'social threat' in the non-Muslim popular imagination. This educator reflected that 'my challenge is wearing a scarf, building self-confidence in my own identity and in being a Muslim'. Not wearing the *hijab* also presented challenges with one educator reporting that:

> when Muslim female parents come in with the *niqab* [full face and body cover] I feel intimidated and 'othered' and feel guilt at the same time because I do not wear a cover and I have the knowledge that in Islam it is wrong.

These educators felt they were vulnerable to diminishing judgements from across cultural interfaces. They were rendered suspect by non-Muslims if they asserted their Muslim identity, and suspect by Muslims if they did not. Furthermore there was little space to celebrate strategic or fluid expressions of identity. The power of hegemonic Western worldviews and practices and its effects in Muslim communities tend to reify cultural practices and view them as bounded and static, while erasing the complexity and diversity within cultures (Keddie, 2012). The risks of compliance or 'epistemic obedience' (Nakata et al., 2012) and 'epistemological closure' (Gordon, 2006: 4) are high. Markers of Islamic identity (such as the *hijab*) have become valorised and universalised by both Muslims and their detractors. This 'single, drastically simplified group identity' (Fraser, 2008: 133) does not account for multiple affiliations and identities. This view of Muslim culture as bounded and universalised was reflected in the data as were attempts to push the boundaries and exercise epistemic 'disobedience'.

The context of Islamophobia also created pressure for educators to conform to Anglo-Australian practices and this resulted in a 'fluidity of practices' (Memon, 2011) as educators moved between communities. However, while it is important to recognise that 'fluidity' of practice was possible and indeed evident, it is also important to acknowledge that it was typically Muslim people who were expected to accommodate cultural differences. Some educators stated that they elected to shake hands with males in the workplace, although this practice was not consistent with their beliefs, or with their practices in the Muslim community, because they did not want to be seen 'to show any discrimination in the workplace'. This practice is consistent with Zine's (2006: 247) study which found that Muslim girls were conscious of not behaving in ways that would be interpreted as rude.

Furthermore, educators in Fatima's study felt that every day early childhood pedagogical practices such as engaging in conversations about big ideas with children sometimes became unsafe under the gaze of Islamophobia, which further compromised their professional identities. For example, Muslim educators who wore the *hijab* stated that one of their challenges in the workplace was answering questions about the *hijab* or Islam posed by children and their families.

Fluidity and hybridity in approaches to pedagogies

The first phase of the action research in Oznur's study involved discussions with Muslim teachers about their struggles with their government mandated requirements to deliver music curriculum. Interview data indicated that these teachers initially believed they had 'no music' in their childhoods and that they grappled with seeing themselves as 'knowing' music. They did, however, remember childhood lullabies in Arabic but these musical experiences had not been reflected or valued in their Western educations. Consequently, the Muslim teachers had constructed their professional identities as music teachers at the fringes, if not outside the boundaries, of teaching music as defined by the state mandated curriculum.

These educators, all of whom had teaching qualifications from Australia, had constructed their teacher identities within the Western epistemologies and pedagogies in Australian initial teacher education programmes. This was reinforced and circumscribed by Australian education policies and curriculum documents which in the perception of the teachers do not engage the worldviews of Muslims and take for granted particular Western approaches to music.

The educators were faced with the challenge of teaching music within a standardised neo-liberal departmental curricula (with its focus on Western music) while also respecting Muslim beliefs about the value of different kinds of music. The teachers' beliefs about Western and Islamic 'music' were complicated and imbued with the power that circulates between Western knowledge and its Oriental 'other'. On one hand, the dominant epistemologies that position Islamic music as 'non-music' had been taken up by the Muslim teachers in this study. Their perception was that if it is religious or Arabic then it's 'not really music' and that Western music is 'more valuable' than Islamic music in 'musical' terms. However, they also saw music as a 'Western alien thing', as one teacher put it. They felt Western music often fell short of its capacity to be spiritually enriching. From an Islamic perspective, music has its roots embedded in spiritual practice, and songs are a spiritual practice of expressing feelings and music is a vehicle of igniting the heart (in a spiritual sense) and hence manifesting an embodiment of connectedness, peace and oneness. From this perspective they perceive much Western music as ego-driven and materialistic.

Early analysis by the teachers of their own lesson plans found little evidence of music being included in the classrooms. Interviews at the beginning of the action research cycle indicated that this lack of music was due to the teachers' uncertainties as to how to integrate music into the curriculum in accordance with Islamic values. As teachers in a Muslim school, they were concerned that families would not be happy with music being taught, or would be concerned it was not appropriate Islamically. Their fear of offending families and the Islamic community, and of being judged as 'bad Muslims', had contributed to a prevailing perception in the school that there was one correct position in regards to Islamic epistemology and pedagogy. Hassim and Cole-Adams (2010) note that there is a range of family perspectives about music in Australian Muslim communities. These include the prohibition of music except during festivals and weddings, the use of a drum and singing of religious songs, acceptance of any music as long as it is modest and reflects moral decency, or as long as the individual is able to 'regulate his or her own behaviour according to Islamic moral standards' (Hassim and Cole-Adams, 2010: 43).

The opportunity to engage in workshops that explored a range of approaches to music in Muslim schools was the basis for the second phase of the action research. This opened up dialogue about possibilities for teaching music that moved beyond the strictures of traditional Islamic faith and narrow interpretations of Western music. The workshops facilitated conversations among teachers that enabled them to contest taken-for-granted views about the Koran and music, what constitutes music and where and how certain kinds of music transgress spiritual practices. As a result teachers broadened their views of music. Rather than having 'no music', the teachers realised that in fact they all had a rich tradition of music to draw on in their teaching. For example, one teacher said, 'I listen to *Anasheed* Islamic music and was brought up with Arabic music as a child.' Others talked about lullabies from their childhood and realised the potential of using this music in the classroom.

The professional learning workshops transformed teachers' understandings of music so that by the end of the project they were incorporating more of their own musical traditions in the curriculum. They also found ways for children's ideas and experiences, such as their interest in rap, to be included. By opening up the dialogue about the intersections between spirituality and music, the teachers were able to look at the intersections between their home and their school context, and this opened up a palette of epistemologies and pedagogies.

The practitioner research started the conversation and teachers realised that it wasn't as difficult to integrate music into the curriculum as they had initially thought. They were no longer afraid of what the parents or education authorities might think and were more clearly able to think through and articulate their beliefs and practices. Music is now integrated across the curriculum, with a range of Islamic and Western music, although not popular music, allowing for a 'fluidity of practice and multiplicity of interpretation and adaption' (Memon, 2011: 296) while still meeting the mandated curriculum requirements and family and community expectations. The practitioner research project provided time and space for teachers to reflect on and share their knowledge of music, to deconstruct existing practices and to develop their own pedagogical approaches to teaching music in an Islamic school that allowed for fluidity and hybridity.

A safe environment where educators can share dilemmas supports transformative practices and creates a third space for knowledge production

One of the key findings from the overarching research conducted by Jen and Leonie is that collaborative practitioner research provides a safe environment for educators to share work that is 'against the grain'. For Muslim educators a secure and trusting environment where they could engage in reflective conversations and critique was particularly important as they were engaging in difficult inquiries into indices of power that sublimate Islamic epistemologies and people.

The Muslim educators were often caught in 'complex knowledge entanglements' (Nakata et al., 2012: 131) involving Western and Islamic epistemologies and pedagogies, where they are positioned as problematic professionals if they question taken-for-granted assumptions about 'what is a good early childhood educator?' and 'what is a good Muslim educator?'. As Muslim early career teachers, members of the *Habibties* group felt vulnerable as they attempted to negotiate a path that drew on their university learning while also taking account of the realities of being a new teacher. The added dimension of being in an Islamic context, or of being Islamic in a secular context, made negotiating 'university' knowledge even more difficult.

They articulated how teachers in Islamic schools are often insulated in an Islamic enclave that provides them with a shared identity. Islamophobia works to push the enclave closer together and makes it increasingly difficult for it to engage with other educational sectors. The enclave is further compounded by issues of private ownership of Muslim schools and early childhood settings by individuals or powerbrokers within particular Islamic communities. The fear of competition on the one hand and scrutiny on the other can limit possibilities of engagement with other educational communities. In this context a safe environment for articulating dilemmas and constructing new knowledge was of critical importance.

As the academic partners, Leonie and Jen repositioned themselves as 'novices' and 'non-experts' (Said, 1994) and found that there was a shifting of power. This was particularly complex with the *Habibties* group, where the nexus of power relations between academic/practitioner and teacher/student that characterised this research cluster were overlayed with issues of Muslim/non-Muslim worldviews and the uneven power relations between Muslims and non-Muslims. We found that collaborative practitioner research, with academics as critical friends, can make inroads that challenge academic/practitioner, Muslim/non-Muslim and theory/ practice binaries and introduce possibilities for new locally produced knowledge and new professional identities where practitioners are recognised as researchers and knowledge producers.

The collegial support provided by the *Habibties* enabled the dissonance between some aspects of Muslim thought and Western pedagogies to be opened up and later, when the group felt confident, these issues were able to be brought into the public domain, firstly by sharing with other groups in the Collaborative Practitioner Research Project, and later through international conference presentations. Because Fatima and Oznur were insiders investigating their own communities, they found that Muslim educators' voices were more able to be heard than if the research had been conducted by outsiders and that educators were able to speak freely about the issues, concerns and experiences they encountered. The exit interview data revealed that the opportunity to be involved in practitioner research gave a sense of agency and empowerment to Muslim educators.

The *Habibties* acted as an insider Islamic space of inquiry where sensitive issues and concerns could be examined and issues of what constitutes Islamic knowledge and pedagogy could be contested. It was a space where Muslim educators could transcend forces of isolation and Islamophobia to reflect critically on practice dilemmas, engage in the epistemic disobedience necessary to deconstruct the dominant pedagogies of Western education systems, and take steps towards transforming practices and creating new knowledge.

Conclusions and insights gained

To engage productively in practitioner research educators need not only a space where they can transcend forces of isolation and critically reflect on and transform practices but also the time to develop the relationships necessary to feel safe to share dilemmas. This is particularly important for those from marginalised groups who are often taking the greatest risks. Change needs to be taken slowly. It is not possible to shift teachers' practices too far or too quickly from what they know. In Fatima's research, for example, educators initially focused on Islamic practices and responses to Islamophobia. Once they had the opportunity to voice their issues and concerns they were more confident to engage in dialogue and critique and could move forward to focus on pedagogical change, which was the next cycle of the action research. Oznur's research showed that teachers can work collaboratively to make small changes to their epistemologies and pedagogies. Strengthened identities allowed Oznur and her colleagues to see themselves as researchers of their own practices.

Collaborative practitioner research opens up a space for epistemic inquiry and the fluidity of professional identities. The creation of a third space between the academy and the field and between Muslim and non-Muslim educators enables a site for critique and for creative responses to diversity. It provides a safe space to engage in epistemic disobedience and to go beyond this to explore the many 'cultural layers' (Keddie, 2012: 165) and 'complex layers of meaning' (Nakata et al., 2012: 127), which is necessary when working to deconstruct epistemological and cultural assumptions and create new knowledge. As Nakata et al. (2012) argue in relation to indigenous education, there is a need for an awakening to new ideas that take account of the complexities of diverse contexts and new tools and a new language to talk and think about and navigate cultural interfaces.

Both academic and practitioner researchers need to be able to work across boundaries (Manathunga, 2009). This border crossing makes the boundaries more permeable (Keddie, 2012: 166) and creates new possibilities and new knowledge. Moving away from dichotomies, such as Western and Islamic epistemologies and pedagogies, and fixed positions of certainty opens up the potential for the analysis of complexities and diverse views.

> **Ongoing research considerations**
>
> - To what extent do initial teacher education courses 'train' teachers to be epistemically obedient members of the teaching profession?
> - What opportunities can you create to cross boundaries and engage in intercultural dialogue?

References

Australian Bureau of Statistics (2012) *Reflecting a Nation: Stories from the 2011 Census, 2012–2013*. Canberra: ABS. Retrieved from www.abs.gov.au/ausstats/abs@.nsf/Lookup/2071.0main+features902012-2013 (last accessed 24 February 2015).

Bhabha, H. K. (ed.) (1994) *The Location of Culture*. London: Routledge.

Buckingham, J. (2010) *The Rise of Religious Schools*. St Leonards, NSW: Centre for Independent Studies.

de Castell, S. (1993) 'Against the grain: narratives of resistance: editor's introduction', *Canadian Journal of Education*, 18: 185–88.

Dillabough, J. (1999) 'Gender policies and conceptions of the modern teacher. women, identity and professionalism', *British Journal of Sociology of Education*, 20 (3): 373–94.

Dimitriadis, G. (2006) 'On the production of expert knowledge: revisiting Edward Said's work on the intellectual', *Discourse: Studies in the Cultural Politics of Education*, 27 (3): 369–82.

Fraser, N. (2008) 'Rethinking recognition: overcoming displacement and reification in cultural politics', in K. Olsen (ed.), *Adding Insult to Injury: Nancy Fraser Debates her Critics*. London: Verso, pp. 129–41.

Goodfellow, J. and Hedges, H. (2006) 'Practitioner research "centre stage": contexts, contributions and challenges', in L. Keesing-Styles and H. Hedges (eds), *Theorising Early Childhood Practice: Emerging Dialogues*. Castle Hill, NSW: Pademelon Press, pp. 187–207.

Gordon, L. (2006) *Disciplinary Decadence: Living Thought in Trying Times*. Boulder and London: Paradigm Publishers.

Gottschalk, P. and Greenberg, G. (2007) *Islamophobia: Making Muslims the Enemy*. Lanham, MD: Rowman and Littlefield Publishers.

Halafoff, A. (2011) 'Countering Islamophobia: Muslim participation in multifaith networks', *Islam and Christian–Muslim Relations*, 22 (4): 451–67.

Hassen, Y. (2013) 'Making Muslims: the politics of religious identity construction and Victoria's Islamic schools', *Islam and Christian–Muslim Relations*, 24 (4): 501–17.

Hassim, E. and Cole-Adams, J. (2010) *Learning from One Another: Bringing Muslim Perspectives into Australian Schools*. Melbourne: National Centre of Excellence for Islamic Studies, University of Melbourne.

Keddie, A. (2012) 'Schooling and social justice through the lenses of Nancy Fraser', *Critical Studies in Education*, 53 (3): 263–79.

Manathunga, C. (2009) 'Research as an intercultural "contact zone"', *Discourse: Studies in the Cultural Politics of Education*, 30 (2): 165–77.

McKenzie, P., Kos, J., Walker, M. and Hong, J. (2008) *Staff in Australia's Schools, 2007*. Canberra: Department of Education, Employment and Workplace Relations.

Memon, N. (2011) 'What Islamic school teachers want: towards developing an Islamic teacher education programme', *British Journal of Religious Education*, 33 (3): 285–98.

Mignolo, W. (2009) 'Epistemic disobedience, independent thought and decolonial freedom', *Theory, Culture and Society*, 26 (7/8): 159–81.

Nakata, M., Nakata, V., Keech, S. and Bolt, R. (2012) 'Decolonial goals and pedagogies for indigenous studies', *Decolonization: Indigeneity, Education and Society*, 1 (1): 120–40.

Poynting, S. and Mason, V. (2007) 'The resistible rise of Islamophobia: anti-Muslim racism in the UK and Australia before 11 September 2001', *Journal of Sociology*, 43 (1): 61–86.

Pratt, M. L. (1992) *Imperial Eyes: Travel Writing and Transculturation*. London: Routledge.

Rizvi, F. (2004) 'Debating globalization and education after September 11', *Comparative Education*, 40 (2): 157–71.

Rizvi, F. and Lingard, B. (2006) 'Edward Said and the cultural politics of education', *Discourse: Studies in the Cultural Politics of Education*, 27 (3): 293–308.

Saeed, A. (2003) *Islam in Australia*. Sydney: Allen and Unwin.

Said, E. (1994) *Representations of the Intellectual*. New York: Vintage Books.

Skattebol, J. and Arthur, L. M. (2014) 'Collaborative practitioner research: opening a third space for local knowledge production', *Asia Pacific Journal of Education*, 34 (3): 351–65.

Whalley, M., Whittaker, P., Fletcher, C., Thorpe, S., John, K. and Leisten, R. (2004) *National Professional Qualification Centre Leadership*. Corby, Northamptonshire: Pen Green Leadership Centre.

Wiredu, K. (1995) *Conceptual Decolonization in African Philosophy: Four Essays*. Ibadan, Nigeria: Hope Publications.

Young, I. M. (2011) *Justice and the Politics of Difference*. Princeton, NJ: Princeton University Press.

Zembylas, M. (2004) 'The emotional characteristics of teaching: an ethnographic study of one teacher', *Teaching and Teacher Education*, 20 (8): 185–201.

Zine, J. (2006) 'Unveiled sentiments: gendered Islamophobia and experiences of veiling among Muslim girls in a Canadian Islamic school', *Equity and Excellence in Education*, 39 (3): 239–52.

4

WHAT IS PLAY FOR, IN YOUR CULTURE? INVESTIGATING REMOTE AUSTRALIAN ABORIGINAL PERSPECTIVES THROUGH PARTICIPATORY PRACTITIONER RESEARCH

Lyn Fasoli and Alison Wunungmurra

Key words   Aboriginal perspectives; children's play; early childhood education and care; remote Aboriginal communities; practitioner research; participatory research.

Chapter overview

This chapter is based on a small-scale qualitative research project undertaken collaboratively by academics and practitioners that aimed to contribute to a gap in early childhood knowledge regarding young Aboriginal children's play. The project investigated the under-researched area of early childhood play from Australian Aboriginal perspectives, drawing on post-modern and indigenous perspectives to challenge and reconceptualise understandings of children's play and to build capacity to support young Aboriginal children's play. The project led to the development of more culturally appropriate Aboriginal community informed early childhood play resources. The chapter explores challenges and insights gained by the Aboriginal and non-Aboriginal authors as they reflect on their experiences in this participatory practitioner research project. The key themes addressed are concepts of play as culturally and socially constructed, early childhood practice and participatory methods for practitioner research.

Study background

Understandings of children's play in the early childhood field have been dominated by research and practice based primarily on the developmental theories of Piaget and play theories of Parten (Ryan and Grieshaber, 2005). These theories have tended to construct the values and purposes associated with young children's play as universal, natural, innocent and applicable to all children (Kirova, 2010; Ryan and Grieshaber, 2005). Play-based learning pedagogy has become virtually taken for granted in the field of early childhood education (Ailwood, 2002; Fleer, 2003) making it a strong discourse in schools, childcare centres and early childhood education training courses. Given the context of the Northern Territory (NT) of Australia where this research took place and where Aboriginal people make up the majority of the population in the remote Aboriginal communities, it was important that some of these taken for granted assumptions about children's play were problematised. Aboriginal people are only 3 per cent of the total Australian population yet they account for 30 per cent of the NT population (Australian Bureau of Statistics, 2011). As a comparison, the next highest proportion of Aboriginal people (4 per cent) lives in the state of Queensland. On this basis alone, it would be logical to assume that the NT would lead the country in advocacy for the inclusion of Aboriginal perspectives in the education of young children. However, this is not the case.

Since non-Aboriginal people arrived in Australia they have disrupted Aboriginal lives at all levels, including their capacity to support their children and nurture their cultural identities as Aboriginal people (Pocock, 2003). European colonisation, past and present, has contributed to the poor health, education and overall wellbeing of Aboriginal children when compared with their non-Aboriginal peers (Steering Committee for the Review of Government Service Provision, 2011). An ongoing concern is for the loss of Aboriginal control over the early childhood services introduced into their communities (Lowell, 2013; Robinson et al., 2008). Remote Aboriginal communities in the NT are intercultural worlds where Anglo-Australian and Aboriginal cultural values and practices sit side by side. Many Aboriginal families struggle to promote their traditional languages, cultural values and practices in the face of more dominant mainstream institutions, discourses and practices (Frawley and Fasoli, 2012; Lowell, 2013).

When this project, called Talking Pictures, took place, early childhood programmes for children under five years old such as childcare, playgroup and parenting programmes, were relatively new in remote NT Aboriginal communities (Fasoli and Moss, 2007), although preschools for four year olds had been operating in some of the larger remote communities since the 1960s. As more early childhood programmes opened their doors, and local Aboriginal staff were employed to run them, demand for training increased as well. The Batchelor Institute of Indigenous Tertiary Education (BI), where the first author Lyn was employed as a teacher educator and educational researcher, was the provider of choice for many Aboriginal staff, based on its 30-year history of providing both-ways[1] culturally responsive education. As the name suggests, the both-ways philosophy calls for the inclusion of both mainstream and Aboriginal and Torres Strait Islander knowledges and perspectives.

Lyn migrated from America to Australia in the 1970s and took up Australian citizenship soon after she arrived in the NT in 1978. Following Cannella and Viruru's (2004) advice that early childhood education and care has become a colonising force, Lyn has worked to understand how her orientation to research has been shaped by her early childhood pedagogy, experience and privilege. She has worked with Aboriginal people in the NT for over 30 years including as a playgroup leader, childcare worker, teacher and teacher educator and always as a white middle-class English speaking woman of privilege (Cannella and Viruru, 2004). She has aimed to work collaboratively and respectfully with Aboriginal families and children and to contribute to the decolonisation of early childhood education through acknowledging and attempting to address some of the injustices that have occurred through colonisation.

Alison, the second author, is an Australian Aboriginal Dhalangu woman from Gapuwiyak in north-east Arnhem Land. She is currently completing her BEd in early childhood. At the time of the research she was employed to work in a playgroup initiated by her community of Gapuwiyak. The playgroup often operated as a childcare centre and was seen as a strategy to address community concerns about some young children's growth, which had been identified through a previous research project, the Child Growth Project (Campbell et al., 2007) between 2000 and 2002.

When Alison first started working in the playgroup she didn't know what she was getting into. She thought of her job as looking after the children, like a babysitter. But as she started getting more experience she began to understand her role had many layers integrating health, education, development and social wellbeing. When she saw the bigger picture she realised that this role was a huge responsibility.

---

[1]Both-ways is a philosophy of education that 'brings together Indigenous Australian traditions of knowledge and Western academic disciplinary positions and cultural contexts, and embraces values of respect, tolerance and diversity'. See https://rest.batchelor.edu.au/main/both-ways (last accessed 24 February 2015).

Alison and Lyn first met at the Children's Services Expo in Batchelor, the small town outside the capital city of Darwin where the Batchelor Institute is located. Lyn set up a 'research' stall at the Expo to invite interest in collaborating to research views of play. Alison was one of the five students who expressed interest. The letters from her community and one other supported the Talking Pictures project to be funded through the Telstra Foundation.

The research team included Lyn, Alison and Aboriginal and non-Aboriginal early childhood lecturers from the Batchelor Institute as well as an Aboriginal student from the other community involved but not reported on in this chapter. The research team worked together for 18 months to conduct the research in two communities. A reference group that included two Aboriginal and one non-Aboriginal early childhood academic was established and met via teleconference on four occasions over the term of the project to provide advice on elements of the research design, ethics, activities and research outcomes.

Gapuwiyak is a small, very remote Aboriginal community of about 700 people (at the time), comprised of 12 different tribes and located about 220 km from the nearest town of Nhulunbuy in Northeast Arnhem Land (NT). It is accessed by a small airstrip or on mostly unsealed roads. The community was first established in the late 1960s and the school in 1970 (Wunungmurra et al., 2002). Aboriginal residents speak a number of local languages before they speak English, which is used mainly at the school or in dealing with government departments or non-Aboriginal visitors. Alison's mother worked there in the community as a highly respected Aboriginal health worker and inspired Alison to pursue further education.

Theoretical perspectives

In Australia, there has been a slow but steady realisation that early childhood ideology has privileged a western view of the world. In the past, Indigenous children were positioned as deficient when they did not match what was expected as the norm for children in early childhood educational settings. (Fleer, 2004: 54)

Views of indigenous children as deficient persist in Australia's education programmes, including early childhood education (Allard and Sanderson, 2003; Amosa et al., 2007). The Talking Pictures project originated out of a concern for the persistence of this discourse. The project drew on early childhood reconceptualist critiques of mainstream Eurocentric early childhood assumptions about young children's play and learning (Burman, 1994; Cannella and Viruru, 2004). These analyses reveal the limitations of foundational theories associated with young children's play, such as Piaget and Parten, which cannot account for and explain the role and purposes of play within diverse cultures (Ailwood, 2002; Fleer, 1999). The notion of promoting play as universally 'good' for all children is also seen as naïve (Fleer, 1999) because it ignores issues of power and privilege. While play *is* universal in the sense that all children engage in play regardless of culture (Rettig, 1995) it is not universal in the way it is defined, understood, supported or valued across cultures (Fleer, 1999; Johns, 1999). Ailwood (2002) finds a mainstream early childhood view of play particularly problematic because 'its valorised, slogan-like status in early childhood education creates a powerful critique-resistant screen, potentially protecting play from investigation and analysis' (Ailwood, 2002: 1).

Australian Aboriginal early childhood researcher Karen Martin (1999) highlights the need for non-Aboriginal people to learn more about Aboriginal perspectives on children and childhood in order to avoid applying 'inappropriate, non Aboriginal norms for child rearing' (1999: 6). The participatory action research tradition at Batchelor Institute that has involved remote Aboriginal communities in research about their own communities and concerns reflects these views as well. For example, in 1993, with funding from the Bernard van Leer Foundation (BvL), Willsher and Clarke (1995) engaged women from 14 remote Aboriginal communities in action research to investigate formally funded children's services and the kinds of services that could work in their communities. Also funded by BvL, the 'Both Ways' Children's Services Project (Fasoli et al., 2004) collaborated with remote Aboriginal participants to research the development of children's services in their communities. These research initiatives reinforced for institute staff the value of working collaboratively with Aboriginal practitioners and communities to better understand and include their perspectives.

Methodology and project methods

The Talking Pictures project aimed to:

- Understand and promote remote Australian Aboriginal community perspectives on the value and purposes of play for their young children (aged four–eight years).
- Trial a research process for supporting the promotion of remote Aboriginal views on play.

The project was a multi-method, qualitative practitioner inquiry (Goodfellow, 2005) drawing on the principles of participatory research (Bergold and

Thomas, 2012; Cornwall and Jewkes, 1995), elements of visual ethnography (Brooks, 2006) and indigenous research protocols (Henry et al, 2002; Martin, 2003). Its participatory nature extended beyond practitioners to include adults and children in the research activities.

Our project took on the characteristics of a practitioner inquiry which include:

- being critically informed
- having as its goal the development of a deeper understanding of professional practice
- encouraging democratic participation through cooperative research with colleagues/parents
- authentic inquiry that is directed towards the 'social good' of all participants, and
- having elements of reflective practice such as review, reconsideration, meaning-making and thoughtful/purposeful action (Macpherson et al., 2004; McTaggart, 1989; Stremmel, 2002; Wolfendale, 1999 cited in Goodfellow, 2005: 50).

These views resonate with participatory approaches (Bergold and Thomas, 2012) where, rather than being objects of study, practitioners work as co-researchers alongside academic researchers (Blodgett et al., 2011). A participatory approach describes a collection of approaches that incorporate collaboration and are capable of engaging participants' perspectives, especially marginalised voices that are often not heard (Bergold and Thomas, 2012). Such participatory approaches are recommended for enabling practitioners to study their own practices (Brydon-Miller and Maguire, 2009) and can foster the kinds of group thinking, talking and learning that are particularly relevant to research involving Aboriginal people (Martin, 2003).

The project was originally conceived as a participatory action research. As the authors have reflected they have reconsidered this label and now understand the project as aligned to participatory research that 'shifts the emphasis from action and change to collaborative research activities' (Bergold and Thomas, 2012: 192) where Aboriginal perspectives on play were considered alongside mainstream views.

Children were included as participants through visual ethnographic methods. This approach provides 'interesting possibilities for inclusive and collaborative research, collecting a wider range of experiential data, and acknowledges the multi-sensory, pre-textual, and cultural experiences of young children' (Brooks, 2006: 68). Space limits in this chapter allow only a brief overview of children's participation.

Indigenous research approaches highlight the potential of mainstream research practice to colonise and oppress indigenous peoples unless power relations are acknowledged and addressed continuously. The 'repositioning of Indigenous peoples within the construction of research' (Henry et al., 2002: 12), so important to shifting the power relations, can also be enabled through participatory approaches when practitioners are positioned as co-researchers who contribute to the production of knowledge alongside the academic researchers.

Social inequality and power imbalances that regularly occur in research collaborations between universities and communities are highlighted by the Australian Institute of Aboriginal and Torres Strait Islander Studies (2000) and National Health and Medical Research Council Guidelines (2003). Alison's participation as a local Aboriginal co-researcher and practitioner was critical in contributing to more equitable power relations within the research team. From the start she recognised the opportunity that the project provided to enable her to research and promote her community's views on play while providing her with access to mainstream early childhood education and care expectations.

Finally, as a participatory project, the methods chosen sought to enable the involvement of as many community members as possible. According to Cornwall and Jewkes (1995) participation can be viewed on a continuum from 'shallow', where researchers control the process, to 'deep' where 'there is a movement towards relinquishing control and devolving ownership of the process to those whom it concerns' (1995: 1676). In Talking Pictures, researchers and community members exerted varying degrees of control over research processes. In the following sections we discuss some of the ways these power relations played out.

Study description

The participants in the project included seven Aboriginal children aged four to eight years old as photographers of their own play and about 40 community members who were interviewed about their perspectives on play. Only the community of Gapuwiyak is discussed in this chapter however.

Ethical clearance was granted by the Batchelor Institute prior to undertaking the research. Permission and informed consent to conduct research from the relevant community council and the traditional owners was granted during the first visit to the community. The institute-based researchers visited Gapuwiyak for a week, six times, over an 18-month period. Between visits we communicated via telephone, email and fax.

Each component of the research journey contained important opportunities to reflect on research processes and power relationships. For the purposes of this chapter we will focus on community engagement processes only.

Community engagement processes

The original proposal started with conversations among the institute-based academics. The personal relationships they had formed with students and their families provided strong foundations for developing research relationships. The Telstra Foundation was identified as a potential source of funding but the timeline for submitting an application was short. The overall goal of this participatory research was to work collaboratively with Aboriginal families to reflect on children's play. If the research was to be of practical use, an essential element of participatory research with Aboriginal people (Ermine et al., 2004), then participants needed to be involved from the beginning.

Alison's participation began at the Children's Services Expo. She returned to her community to seek their support to participate but after three weeks had gone by and no firm commitment had come, Lyn became anxious because of the approaching deadline for submitting the funding application. She began to make regular telephone calls and to send urgent faxes requesting advice on the community's decision. This kind of pressure is very counterproductive for participants. However, Alison secured the letter of community support, which arrived just in time for the funding to be secured.

Alison has written about the inappropriate pressure to respond to new ideas that non-Aboriginal people often put on Aboriginal communities, likening it to a 'tsunami'.

> People come into communities with new ideas and just scrape the community clean of the old ideas. People in communities already have good ideas about how to fix problems. But this tsunami consultation doesn't listen to those good ideas ... Consultation should be like a raindrop... a new idea drops into the community and spreads out. These ripples are the good idea spreading out through the people, through to the outstations and then coming back again to the centre, making a new space for thinking about the new ideas, combined with the old ideas. (Wunungmurra, 2010: 10)

The inclusion of the children in researching their own play appealed to Alison who thought they would enjoy the experience. We agreed on a plan for introducing them to the research and then held a community meeting. Lyn described the project and Alison translated. From Lyn's perspective the visual methods were designed to provide children with a direct role in data gathering and interpretation and an opportunity to express their views on play (Lansdown, 2004). For Alison, this seemed like an interesting but unfamiliar way to do research that didn't match her earlier experiences as a research assistant on another project. At this point research methods were merely described and agreement sought rather than negotiated, but that soon changed.

Orderly research plans and assumptions began to unravel as they often do in participatory research (Cornwall and Jewkes, 1995). At the community meeting everyone had appeared to agree with the premise that only four child photographers were needed because we only had four cameras. Lyn believed she had negotiated these selection criteria as a fair way to select child photographers:

- aged between four and eight years
- able to physically manage the cameras
- chose freely to participate and displayed a strong interest in play
- cooperative
- represented a gender balance
- represented all family groups and clans in the community.

Clearly these criteria reflect many mainstream assumptions about fairness. Categorisation by age is used routinely to organise children in mainstream education. Despite her stated intention to provide children with voice and opportunity, on reflection, Lyn could see these criteria were boundaries for containing and controlling how children used the cameras. They also echoed familiar mainstream child management strategies designed to focus children on their roles as photographers. To make this management strategy even more tangible to the young children a small badge on a lanyard had been designed to identify the wearer as an 'approved' photographer and to distinguish child photographers from other children. Alison recalls going along with Lyn on many of these earlier activities. For example, Alison only mentioned after the meeting that only one of the clan groups had been present when these criteria were negotiated. Rather than raise the issue of clan representation at the time, she spent the rest of the day recruiting children from different clans. When a much larger group than four children arrived, jumping with excitement and ready to get started, Lyn was confused as well as surprised. Alison took the lead. She talked to the group of about 20 children in their own language about what they were to do. Within minutes they were ready to begin. This large group of child photographers ended up freely swapping cameras and badges, melding the research imposed rules with their own. Alison explained that they had their own rules and ways of sharing according to kinship relationships that Lyn did not fully understand but which Alison approved. Alison took on board the importance of including children from each clan group as a way to ensure that the whole community was engaged and benefited but, at this point, she chose an indirect way to solve the problem rather than discuss it with Lyn.

As we talked together and went about the business of doing the research we began to develop a closer and more trusting relationship that enabled more shared understanding of what was going on. We were developing what Reason (2004) calls a 'communicative space' that allowed us to explore differences and similarities in our thinking. Alison was able to voice her awareness and concern that her playgroup was also not always engaging all of the families in the community, indicating this issue as something she wanted to address. Hearing about the challenges confronting remote Aboriginal people in small communities where very few jobs were available to them, Lyn began to understand how access to work, including the work of being a paid co-researcher as Alison was, was a privilege that could set her apart from some members of her community and impact on her capacity to engage the community as a whole. The conversations we had around this time were tentative at first, but slowly developed more depth and honesty. The development of a safe communicative space for sharing issues, confusions, insights and new questions must be continuously negotiated (Bergold and Thomas, 2012).

Alison began to take a more active role in directing and adapting the research processes and Lyn began to trust that the research processes that emerged from their collaboration would result in more community-appropriate ways of working leading to better and wider engagement. As Bergold and Thomas (2012) point out, 'Role distribution in participatory research is not static. Rather, it is subject to continual change' (2012: 203). The involvement of adult interviewees was an example of this process. The first adults we interviewed were the parents of the children who had taken the photographs. Through their children's involvement they were already interested in contributing. Other adults were interviewed as we walked around the community with 15 of the children's photographs, showing them to groups and individuals. Standard approaches to informed consent rarely occurred. While we attempted to follow appropriate ethical protocols, so keen were some people to contribute that they did not attend to the plain language statement or sign the consent form. They simply started putting their views forward.

We justify this by making the ethical case that discussing consent after the interview, when an interviewee is more aware of what the research is all about, enables a more thorough understanding of possible ethics issues. If a person is uncomfortable with the interview process after the interview, no consent needs to be given as the interview will not be used.

Adult interviewees responded strongly to the photographs. The children's play images recalled their own play experiences as children. As they reminisced, they clearly identified the importance that their play had had for their learning, especially for the cultural knowledge they gained through playing alongside adults as they went about their activities. These interviews were managed, primarily by Alison, as group discussions rather than traditional interviews. While she translated for Lyn, often the conversation went on for long periods without Lyn knowing what was being said. These experiences clearly illustrate how the power relations had shifted between us as researchers. Later each evening she would translate the tapes explaining what people said.

Adults emphasised how times had changed. People observed that there were fewer opportunities than in the past to take children 'out bush' to go hunting. More families were sitting around the TV rather than the campfire. Many of the grandmothers, whose traditional role was to ensure children's cultural learning, had poor health or had too many grandchildren to look after. Alison's involvement in these discussions prompted her to reflect on her role as an early childhood leader who could use these research insights to foster play for the cultural as well as the education and health reasons previously identified by her community.

Conclusions and insights gained

This chapter has described the Talking Pictures project, a participatory research project undertaken by academic researchers working collaboratively with Aboriginal practitioner co-researchers and their communities to share knowledge about Aboriginal children's play. We have reflected on the development of a communicative space that enabled the research to become more truly collaborative, where researchers worked out 'what to do', as Reason (2004: 3) puts it. The trust and communication we developed led to more research flexibility and more give and take in our roles as co-researchers. During the

(Continued)

(Continued)

early phase of relationship building, neither Alison nor the other parents directly challenged Lyn about some of the proposed research processes (for example, selecting child photographers), yet they found ways to resist them. Lyn constantly referred to indigenous research protocols in order to be able to recognise these moments as times for reflection and flexibility rather than react negatively. An important orientation for Lyn from the beginning of the research was a stance as learner as well as researcher. Alison moved significantly in the other direction from learner to researcher. She began to look at the research process less as a set of technical skills to be learned, as if she was a research assistant, and more as an opportunity to reflect on issues of importance to her and to her community and to negotiate around important research decisions.

   Working in a safe communicative space we could each step back from leading the research when uncertain of how to proceed. In that pause created by each other's uncertainty, the other could step forward to suggest alternatives and solutions. The research ethics application may have stated that indigenous research protocols would drive all aspects of the research but this still required constant attention to what this meant in practice. According to Bergold and Thomas (2012) participatory research processes are good contexts for enabling this kind of give and take to happen. 'The participatory research process enables co-researchers to step back cognitively from familiar routines, forms of interaction, and power relationships in order to fundamentally question and rethink established interpretations of situations and strategies' (2012: 192).

Ongoing research considerations

- What challenges and opportunities are offered by the concept of a communicative space for supporting research relationships between practitioners and academics undertaking collaborative research?
- How do you (or could you) engage your own local community as participants in a research project?
- How could the example of participation offered in this chapter contribute to more participatory forms of parent engagement in your children's schooling or childcare?

References

Ailwood, J. (2002) 'Homogenising play: governing preschool childhoods', paper presented at the Australian Association for Research in Education Annual Conference, Brisbane. Retrieved from: www.aare.edu.au/02pap/ail02210.htm (last accessed 12 May 2006).

Allard, A., and Sanderson, V. (2003) 'Whose school? Which community?', *Education in Rural Australia*, 13 (1): 41–62.

Amosa, W., Ladwig, J., Griffiths, T. and Gore, J. (2007) 'Equity effects of quality teaching: closing the gap', paper presented at the Australian Association for Research in Education Annual Conference, Fremantle, WA. Retrieved from: www.aare.edu.au/07pap/amo07284.pdf (last accessed 12 July 2013).

Australian Bureau of Statistics (2011) *Estimates of Aboriginal and Torres Strait Islander Australians*, June (cat. no. 3238.0.55.001). Canberra: ABS. Retrieved from: www.abs.gov.au/ausstats/abs@.nsf/mf/3238.0.55.001 (last accessed 13 August 2014).

Australian Institute of Aboriginal and Torres Strait Islander Studies (2000) *Guidelines for Ethical Research in Indigenous Studies*. Canberra: AIATSIS.

Bergold, J. and Thomas, S. (2012) 'Participatory research methods: a methodological approach in motion', *Historical Social Research*, 37 (4): 191–222.

Blodgett, A. T., Schinke, R. J., Smith, B., Peltier, D. and Pheasant, C. (2011) 'In Indigenous words: exploring vignettes as a narrative strategy for presenting the research voices of Aboriginal community members', *Qualitative Inquiry*, 17 (6): 522–33.

Brooks, M. (2006) 'Using visual ethnography in the primary classroom', *Australian Research in Early Childhood Education*, 13 (2): 67–80.

Brydon-Miller, M. and Maguire, P. (2009) 'Participatory action research: contributions to the development of practitioner inquiry in education', *Educational Action Research*, 17 (1): 79–93.

Burman, E. (1994) *Deconstructing Developmental Psychology*. London: Routledge.

Campbell, D., Pyett, P. and McCarthy, L. (2007) 'Community development interventions to improve Aboriginal health: building an evidence base', *Health Sociology Review*, 16 (3–4): 304–14.

Cannella, G. and Viruru, R. (2004) *Childhood and Postcolonization: Power, Education, and Contemporary Practice*. New York: RoutledgeFalmer.

Cornwall, A., and Jewkes, R. (1995) 'What is participatory research?', *Social Science Medical Journal*, 41 (2): 1667–76.

Ermine, W., Sinclair, R. and Jeffery, B. (2004) *The Ethics of Research Involving Indigenous Peoples: Report of the Indigenous Peoples' Health Research Centre to the Interagency Advisory Panel on Research Ethics*. Retrieved from: http://ahrnets.ca/files/2010/05/ethics_review_iphrc.pdf (last accessed 22 May 2015).

Fasoli, L. and Moss, B. (2007) 'What can remote indigenous child care teach us?', *Contemporary Issues in Early Childhood*, 8 (3): 265–74.

Fasoli, L., with Benbow, R., Deveraux, K., Falk, I., Harris, R., James, R., Johns, V., Preece, C. and Railton, K. (2004) *'Both Ways' Children's Services Project*. Batchelor, NT: Batchelor Press.

Fleer, M. (1999) 'Universal fantasy: the domination of Western theories of play', in E. Dau (ed.), *Child's Play: Revisiting Play in Early Childhood Settings*. Sydney: Maclennan and Petty Priority Limited, pp. 67–80.

Fleer, M. (2003) 'Early childhood education as an evolving "community of practice" or as lived "social reproduction": researching the "taken-for-granted"', *Contemporary Issues in Early Childhood*, 4 (1): 64–79.

Fleer, M. (2004) 'The cultural construction of early childhood education: Creating institutional and cultural intersubjectivity', paper presented at the XXIV World Congress of OMEP, Melbourne, Australia, July.

Frawley, J. and Fasoli, L. (2012) 'Working together: intercultural leadership capabilities for both-ways education', *School Leadership and Management: Formerly School Organisation*, 32 (4): 309–20.

Goodfellow, J. (2005) 'Researching With/For Whom? Stepping in and out of Practitioner Research', *Australian Journal of Early Childhood*, 30(4): 48–57.

Henry, J., Dunbar, T., Arnott, A., Scrimgeour, M., Matthews, S., Murakami-Gold, L. and Chamberlain, A. (2002) *Indigenous Research Reform Agenda: Rethinking Research Methodologies* (Links Monograph Series : 2). Darwin: Cooperative Research Centre for Aboriginal and Tropical Health.

Johns, V. (1999) 'Embarking on a journey: Aboriginal children and play', in E. Dau (ed.), *Child's Play: Revisiting Play in Early Childhood Settings*. Sydney: MacLennan and Petty Priority Limited, pp. 60–6.

Kirova, A. (2010) 'Children's representations of cultural scripts in play: facilitating transition from home to preschool in an intercultural early learning program for refugee children', *Diaspora, Indigenous and Minority Education*, 4 (2): 74–91.

Lansdown, G. (2004) 'Participation of young children', *Early Childhood Matters*, 103 (November): 4–14.

Lowell, A. (2013) '"From your own thinking you can't help us": intercultural collaboration to address inequities in services for indigenous Australians in response to the World Report on Disability', *International Journal of Speech-Language Pathology*, 15 (1): 101–05.

Macpherson, I., Brooker, R., Aspland, T. and Cuskelly, E. (2004) 'Constructing a territory for professional practice research: some introductory considerations', *Action Research*, 2 (1): 89–106.

Martin, K. (1999) 'When "why?" becomes "why not?": cultural safety and Aboriginal early childhood services', *Every Child*, 5 (4): 6–7.

Martin, K. (2003) 'Indigenous research – a communal act', paper presented at the Joint Australian Association for Research in Education (AARE) and New Zealand Association for Research in Education (NZARE) Conference, Auckland. Retrieved from: www.aare.edu.au/data/publications/2003/her03635. pdf (last accessed 24 February 2015).

McTaggart, R. (1989) '16 tenets of participatory action research'. Retrieved from: http://caledonia.org.uk/par.htm (last accessed 17 December 2004).

National Health and Medical Research Council (2003) *Values and Ethics: Guidelines for Ethical Conduct in Aboriginal and Torres Strait Islander Health Research*. Canberra: NHMRC.

Pocock, J. (2003) *State of Denial: The Neglect and Abuse of Indigenous Children in the Northern Territory*. Melbourne: SNAICC. Retrieved from: www.snaicc. asn.au/_uploads/rsfil/01836.pdf (last accessed 24 February 2015).

Reason, P. (2004) 'Action research: forming communicative space for many ways of knowing. Response to Md. Anisur Rahman', paper presented at the International Workshop on Participatory Action Research, Dhaka, 3 March.

Rettig, M. (1995) 'Play and cultural diversity', *The Journal of Educational Issue of Language Minority Students*, 15. Retrieved from: www.ncela.gwu.edu/pubs/ jeilms/vol15/playandc.htm (2 September 2007).

Robinson, G., Eickelkamp, U., Goodnow, J. and Katz, I. (2008) *Contexts of Child Development Culture, Policy and Intervention*. Darwin: Charles Darwin University Press.

Ryan, S., and Grieshaber, S. (2005) *Practical Transformations and Transformational Practices: Globalization, Postmodernism, and Early Childhood Education*. Oxford: Elsevier.

Steering Committee for the Review of Government Service Provision (SCRGSP) (2011) *Overcoming Indigenous Disadvantage: Key Indicators 2011*. Canberra: Productivity Commission.

Stremmel, A. (2002) 'Nurturing professional and personal growth through inquiry', *Young Children*, 57 (5): 62–70.

Willsher, M. and Clarke, M. (1995) *Talking Early Childhood: A Profile of Services and Programs for Young Aboriginal Children Living on Remote Communities in the Northern Territory*. Batchelor, NT: Batchelor College.

Wolfendale, S. (1999) 'Parents as partners in research and evaluation: methodological and ethical issues and solutions', *British Journal of Special Education*, 26 (3): 164–9.

Wunungmurra, A. (2010) 'Authentic consultation – like a raindrop, not a tsunami', *SNAICC News*, March. Retrieved from: http://www.snaicc.org.au/_uploads/ rsfil/02541.pdf (last accessed 22 May 2015).

Wunungmurra, A. D., Manamirra, S., Wunungmurra, R. Y., Djeliyarrawuy, S., Gupumpu, L., Walambi, M., Wunungmurra, D., Wunungmurra, A. M. and Munungurr, D. W. (2002) *Gapuwiyak Dhawu: A History of the North East Arnhem Land Community*. Batchelor, NT: Batchelor Press.

5

DEVELOPING COLLABORATION USING MIND MAPS IN PRACTITIONER RESEARCH IN SWEDEN

Karin Rönnerman

Key words   practitioner research; mind map method; collaborative analyses.

Chapter overview

This chapter discusses Swedish early childhood teacher teams working as practitioner researchers to improve the quality of their work. The early childhood teachers implemented mind-mapping techniques to enquire into their own practices with the author with whom they have previously studied a course in action research (Rönnerman, 2008). Two of the teachers were employed as mentors (Edwards-Groves and Rönnerman, 2013), using generative leadership by facilitating groups of colleagues from different schools in action research (Rönnerman, 2011). Contact with the university researcher, and participation in seminars and a research circle focusing on their role as peer leaders in nurturing practitioner research (Rönnerman and Olin, 2014,) are ongoing features of their shared work.

The focus here is the experience of collaborative mind-mapping. However, the method also aimed at teaching the practitioners how to develop deeper knowledge about their practices. The focus questions are a) how do practitioners value taking part in collaborative research? and b) do practitioners find the method useful in their own research? In this chapter I argue that one way to strengthen the relationship between theory and proven experiences for practitioners is through their involvement in collaborative action research where they are able to discuss (and analyse) their own practices with university researchers, and become active in analysing, understanding and reflecting on their own practice. The findings suggest that practitioners benefit from tools that support them to gain a deeper understanding of their practice in order to be able to change it, and that the teachers used various words to talk about their practice that can be described in terms of professional knowledge.

The chapter begins with a brief description of the Swedish early childhood education system, followed by an overview of collaborative action research as it has developed in relation to the Nordic tradition of folk enlightenment (in Swedish, *folkbildning*). There follows a detailed presentation of the research method. Focusing on the two questions above, the results of a follow-up survey sent to the practitioners involved is discussed. The chapter concludes with a discussion about the importance of teachers visualising their work collaboratively in order to gain a deeper understanding of their practices and how this knowledge could contribute to them researching their own practices. The key themes are collaborative practitioner research, mind map method and collaborative analyses. Readers can expect to learn how one early childhood centre collaboratively investigated and analysed their own work to gain deeper understanding.

Early childhood education – the first step in the Swedish national education system

Early childhood education is the first level of the Swedish education system, and since 1998 has had its own curriculum. Learning and quality have become major concepts in the discourses of early childhood education and are even more highly emphasised in the revised curricula of 2011 (Skolverket, 2014). Unlike teachers in schools, early childhood teachers are not supposed to judge students' performance, but to critically investigate the environment and how it can be developed in order to promote children's learning and development. To develop the environment to meet children's development and learning needs, teachers' own professional learning has to be in the foreground; however, the teachers' understanding of these processes is rarely emphasised.

By law, municipalities in Sweden should provide early childhood education for children from the age of one, if parents are working or studying, are unemployed or are on leave of absence from work. From the age of three, all children have free access to early childhood education for 525 hours per year. Table 5.1 shows that the majority of children in Sweden attend early childhood education (Skolverket, 2011).

Early childhood education centres in Sweden have their own buildings, like schools, divided into different units. With approximately 20 children per unit, the children are grouped either in similar age levels or in mixed age groups. Each unit has a teacher team of three–four people, of whom at least two are qualified teachers with university degrees, and the others with upper secondary school qualifications. The centres are open for 12 hours per day and encompass both education and care (educare). Quality in early childhood education was first given attention at a national level in 2005, and as a result of the Education Act (1 July 2011), principals at each early childhood centre are responsible for quality and working in collaboration with the early childhood teachers (Education Act, 2011). A recently released report by the School Inspection Team (Skolinspektionen, 2012), details recommendations from the investigation of 42 centres in 14 different municipalities. Two out of the four recommendations noted that improving quality has to be part of everyday work and that quality leadership has to be strengthened, especially among the early childhood teachers (Skolinspektionen, 2012: 3).

The inspection also requires that teachers take part in the development of everyday activities and act as leaders or practitioner researchers. This stance can also be found in the Education Act (2011), emphasising the need for early childhood education to be built on science and proven experiences, meaning early childhood teachers need to be more aware of theoretical knowledge in their work. Two of the early childhood teachers

Table 5.1 Proportion of children enrolled in early childhood education, divided by age group

Municipality	proportion (%) of children enrolled in early childhood education in Sweden						
	1–5 years old	0 year old	1 year old	2 year old	3 year old	4 year old	5 year old
All municipalities	83	0	48	88	93	94	94

involved as mentors in the study have facilitated their peers in action research for almost ten years, with a view to improving quality in early childhood education, maintaining contact with the university researcher over this time, and inviting the development of collaboration with the university researcher in this new project.

Theoretical framing and research within the field

The theories used in the research are deeply rooted in the Nordic tradition of action research, with a specific emphasis on knowledge building through regular involvement in group meetings where communication is through democratic dialogues, and is highly valued.

Collaboration and dialogue

Research shows that teachers make a difference to children's learning (Hattie, 2011; Timperley, 2011). This recognition has led to an emphasis on collaborations between teachers in order to develop and improve pedagogical practice, leading to improvements in students' development, learning and achievement. Practitioner research, with its focus on professional development and improvement of practice, often involves collaboration and partnerships with university researchers (Groundwater-Smith et al., 2012). An established partnership between schools and universities, and other forms of collaboration with academics, aims to create meetings on equal terms in which both theoretical and practical knowledge are used and valued. To reach such an understanding, creating spaces for communication and dialogue is essential.

Examination of two prominent handbooks of action research (Noffke and Somekh, 2009; Reason and Bradbury, 2001) reveals frequent use of concepts such as participation, cooperation, community and collaboration. Collaboration and collegial work is also highly emphasised in international studies by Hattie (2011) and Timperley (2011), providing evidence that collaborative approaches lead to an increase in students' learning and development. However, these studies seldom problematise how this collaboration can take place or what tools are needed to nurture a dialogue among practitioners.

Emphasising a democratic dialogue in collaborative forums can be linked to the Nordic traditions of *bildung* (*bildning* in Swedish) and folk enlightenment (*folkbildning*). Beginning in the 1930s in Sweden, folk enlightenment was formed as a collaborative practice for the working classes, aiming to make sense of the social, political and structural changes taking place in the society (Larsson and Nordvall, 2010). A specific form, the 'study circle', was established and used in workplaces, promoting adult education and enabling workers to collaboratively discuss literature with the purpose of becoming active citizens. The study circles developed into research circles in the 1970s, when universities were asked by the Labour union to collaborate in leading circles to understand the societal changes occurring, e.g. the crises in the shipbuilding and car industries (Holmer, 1993; Holmstrand and Härnsten, 2003). The study circle and later the research circle were used as an ideal form for meeting in small groups and as a collaborative approach to discussions, with focus questions decided upon by the participants (Rönnerman and Salo, 2012). Furthermore, these circles enhanced participants' better understanding of their situation and ways of eliciting the knowledge to change it. Usually they involved a problem that was jointly decided, and which should be scrutinised from different perspectives by using the participants' experiences, together with theoretical perspectives contributed by the university researcher. The intention is not to solve the problem but to inquire into it and thereby to widen the participants' knowledge about it. A study or research circle is not a uniform concept but can be described as a meeting in which participants conduct an organised search for, and development of, knowledge in cooperation with other participants. The process of developing knowledge can be seen in three ways: as gaining knowledge, as developing participants' capability and as participating in the social production of knowledge (Holmer, 1993).

Based on this Nordic tradition in adult education, structures supporting collaboration between university researchers and practitioner researchers have been further developed in collaborative action research (Rönnerman et al., 2008; Rönnerman and Salo, 2012, Rönnerman and Salo, 2014). Most common are research circles (Holmstrand and Härnsten, 2003), used frequently in early childhood education (Enö, 2005; Rönnerman and Olin, 2014). Similarly, in Norway and Sweden, dialogue conferences have been taken up as a way of dealing with new reforms in schools (Furu and Lund, 2014; Lund, 2008) and creating spaces for sharing knowledge between all parties (teachers, leaders, etc.) at a workplace, aiming at democratic dialogues for improvement.

Gustavsen (2001) refers to democratic dialogue as the most important element when working for change in organisations. He argues against implementing theory-driven approaches as they limit the participation of the actors, with the risk of them becoming only doers in practice. To overcome this dualism between theory and practice he suggests a third discourse, a mediating discourse, which links theory with practice. He argues that putting the dialogue into the foreground will promote the theory–practice link. Gustavsen further emphasises the necessity of integrating disagreement, and continuously generating decisions that provide a platform for joint action, or challenges. With this design, relationship building is at the fore rather than single product events (Gustavsen, 2001: 22, Table 1.1), and by sharing experiences from different departments, participants learn more about the whole process.

This emphasis on collaboration and democratic dialogues can quite easily be found in today's debate about successful school development. Teacher Learning Communities (TLC) (McLaughlin and Talbert, 2006) and Professional Learning Communities (PLC) (Stoll et al., 2006) are among those frequently used. Wenger's (1998) work in relation to communities of practice is also an example of collective learning being developed by teachers discussing children's development, learning and achievement in relation to various factors in early childhood education and school.

The approach taken in this study, of involving practitioners in jointly constructing mind maps, can be viewed as a community approach, building on the Nordic tradition of study/research circles, as we had the purpose of democratically deepening, sharing, developing and constructing new knowledge (Holmer, 1993) for further actions.

Methodology

In this section I describe the mind map method and how the five step method was used with the four early childhood teacher teams. Based on the study's framing of collaboration, a strong aim was to elaborate how to produce data that would provide insights and benefits for the practitioners involved. The approach taken builds on experiences from a previous study, where group interviews were used for graphic presentations inspired by mind maps (Gannerud and Rönnerman, 2005). Mind maps are typically used as a way of taking notes or sorting and categorising thinking. In this and the previous study they were instead used as a way of visualising the dialogue by writing on Post-It notes and by formulating cluster statements on different themes as a way of capturing teachers' work. The mind map experience built on a connection to everyday practice, created a good interaction between university researchers and practitioner researchers, and facilitated teachers' own expressions about their everyday work being visualised in an effective and clear way (Gannerud and Rönnerman, 2005). The mind map technique was combined with group interviews with the teams. Teachers were involved in the group interviews and took an active role in the repeated analyses.

Practitioners' collaboration in constructing mind maps

Four teams from one four-unit early childhood centre participated. The teams (three–five persons) included early childhood teachers, child minders and teachers with another mother tongue than Swedish. Not all teachers were present at all occasions due to part-time work or starting later on the particular day that meetings were held. The teams met with the two university researchers five times over five months, during which the mind map was constructed, analysed and finalised. The meetings focused on how professional development and leadership were nurtured in the early childhood centre, based on the teachers' knowledge and development of practitioner research for quality in their work. A year later the teachers were surveyed with six questions about their experiences of participating in the project. Six early childhood teachers answered the survey. In the following section the process of constructing the mind maps and the repeated analyses are described. The results from the survey will be presented in the subsequent section.

Collaborative construction: a mind map in five steps

The process of constructing the mind maps can be described as including:

- conversations with teacher teams about their professional learning and about leading practitioner research
- university researchers interchangeably asking and following up questions, writing answers and constructing clusters in themes on the paper
- collaborative construction of the mind map through dialogues to visualise the conversation
- reorganising (analysing) the mind map in five analytic steps as described below.

The conversation with each team started with an open question (about professional development and leadership), asking simply, 'What projects are going on at this early childhood centre?' Based on the answers, new questions were used focusing on the practitioners' professional development and leadership within the centre. During the meeting the teachers were asked to describe their individual views on professional development, but to avoid a consensus perspective, so as to get as many nuances as possible. The mind map was constructed at the first meeting (step 1) and analysed with the practitioners in four further steps (outlined below). All meetings were audio recorded and lasted for about two hours. The five separate steps detail the structure:

1. The teacher team met with two university researchers around a table on which a sheet of butcher paper was placed. At first the teachers were simply asked to describe their work, what projects were going on and what they thought had influenced them. While the teachers were speaking, one of the researchers kept the conversation going and the other wrote their statements with specific phrases written as keywords on Post-It notes. Post-Its were grouped and re-grouped by themes, as the need arose. After about 15–20 minutes one of the researchers stopped the discussion to look at the stickers and emerging themes on the sheet. The researchers asked questions about concepts clustered together and new questions were asked about how the words were organised into themes, should any be moved or if other concepts should be added. This was a time for reflection to enable the teachers to observe the pattern and move stickers around. During the meeting two such pauses for reflections were made. When finished, the big, rather messy, sheet was rolled up, together with all its Post-Its, and taken back to the university. The university researchers then started to reconstruct the mind map, putting the statements together in different clusters like a mind map. Some of the theme bubbles were left without a heading as a way of encouraging the practitioners to name them based on their experiences and words.

2. When presented with the rewritten mind map, the practitioners expressed surprise, commenting on how much they were doing and how things hung together. The practitioners were asked to label the empty bubbles and to comment further on the picture. The university researchers were very conscious of trying to get the teachers to name the clusters with 'their' concepts on specific themes and phenomena visualised on the reconstructed mind map. The teachers also added missing areas to construct a more complete picture of their work, as well as being invited to move activities between clusters so that the mind map would cover their work as completely as possible. The university researchers then remodelled the mind map a second time, with a focus on professional development and leadership. This construction of the mind map ended up as three circles labelled with overarching concepts: 'continuing professional development', 'practice' and 'teacher team'. In each corner of the sheet, around the three circles, external prerequisites were recorded. These external prerequisites were 'action research', 'the principal', 'the development leader', 'different meetings', as these had come up during the conversations and were used as the starting point in the third session.

3. The elaborated mind map was presented to the teacher teams and they were asked to speak about how they identified external conditions

as influencing their work. While speaking about this, lines or arrows were drawn on the reconstructed mind map to visualise how these external conditions influenced and were connected with one another, e.g. how CPD courses in action research had influenced their work to be more inquiry-based and systematic, but also how a teacher within one of the teams had taken on a leading role as a mentor, facilitating the other teams within the centre to promote practitioner research.

4.   In the fourth step, the mind maps were graphically rewritten by the university researchers and ended up as three boxes, each representing professional development, practice and teacher teams. 'Practice' was put in the middle, and the teacher team described their work with the children as everyday activities. The teachers mentioned specific activities but also expressed their ideas in terms of different goals: for example, how to make learning visible for the individual child or how to increase the children's influence over activities. Those expressions were connected to professional knowledge by the university researchers. The left box, 'professional development', contained activities that were sometimes required by the principal, such as attending special lectures, visits to other schools or reading some specific literature. However, more often the teachers pointed out that the initiative had come from them and the principal had merely carried through the organisation of it. From the mind map, it was obvious that action research had an impact on ongoing professional development and had made an important contribution to how this early childhood centre was developing. When collaboratively analysing what and how the teachers spoke about the work of the teacher team, two kinds of activities appeared. One was more obvious: planning daily activities by structuring work for children's learning. The other was activities that the teachers described as promoting their professional learning, which they explained as actions followed in a systematic way (action research). They mentioned discussions based on documentations/observations, giving and receiving critical comments on each other's work, discussing the value of new ideas (their own or others) for specific actions, testing new ideas and listening carefully to each other's experiences.

5.   At the beginning of the following semester, the university researchers returned to the early childhood centre to present an overview of the whole data collection and the processes written out as a time line over the previous semester. The teachers were asked to comment on the full process, and how it had affected any aspect of their work. All four teacher teams received a copy of their mind maps with their different steps.

Survey findings

The findings are based on the answers to the survey from the six participating teachers. Specific categories were established by reading the answers over and over again and are presented together with excerpts from the teachers' written answers, to allow their voices to be heard (Kvale, 1998). The answers are divided into two main categories: 'collaboration and learning' and 'benefits and consequences' from being part of a collaborative action research project.

Collaboration and learning

When the teachers looked back on the process of taking part they emphasised collaboration in various ways. The analysis shows how the teachers' responses reveal that collaboration was viewed from two perspectives: 'within the teacher team' and 'with the researchers'.

Collaboration within the teacher team

Firstly, the teachers talked about collaboration in connection with coming together as a team. In this context the teachers frequently used expressions such as 'inspiring', 'challenging', 'deepening knowledge' and 'a way to increase a feeling of being a team'. The following quotes are examples of the teachers' responses:

> We got an increased sense of belonging in the team. (Teacher 3)

> The collaboration was good because the things we had done were highlighted and then you see how much we are doing. (Teacher 5)

Although the teachers work as a team and have regular meetings they found it highly satisfying coming together to use time just to focus on their own practices in the discussions.

The answers show how discussing their joint work together in the team strengthened the team. The teachers explained that they had opportunities to express their own thoughts on specific matters and were able to contribute to their colleagues' ideas. This process was emphasised as a way of sharing and getting deeper knowledge about their joint practices, when everybody could take part in the conversation and everybody's thinking and opinions were 'on the table' in the discussions. During the discussions in the mind map meetings, the teachers were also able to see, when talking, how expressions of their practice were growing as clusters on the sheet of paper leading to the construction of the mind map. The teachers emphasised the importance of visualising what they were doing in survey responses: 'it gives you a new dimension on your work'. This is further emphasised in the following quotes:

> When we sat together it was an incredible feeling to be able to see how much we are doing that we are not aware of. (Teacher 2)

> Our work was visible in the organisation. Work with the children, for parents, for the principal, in the municipality, planning our work and all cooperation in preschool and our skills. (Teacher 4)

By allowing all participants to see the same pattern, to be able to put their own views into words, and to further reflect on it, they were all included and sharing a creative conversation. In the next quotes two teachers further elaborate on the effects of this work:

> It strengthened the team and everyone got a chance in their own way to express their thoughts. By that, new ideas were created and provided a deeper insight into our work. (Teacher 3)

> Good for everyone to participate and talk about our practice and what we are doing. (Teacher 6)

The visualisation of a mind map also points at certain aspects that are normally taken for granted and are not discussed or even mentioned as work. This was particularly evident for aspects not related to the work with the children, but that obviously take time and are part of the work-load, for example collaboration with other professionals. By structuring the mind map, the teachers became aware of their work and its totality and complexity. In the next quote one of the teachers gives further details:

> We got it up and made ideas visible, practices and structures, strengths and weaknesses of the common work. Saw the complexity of our work, how it all hangs together, what permeates our school and that we are skilled! Stuff you rarely have time to sit and discuss ... A very useful method! Important to have time to sit together undisturbed, do follow-ups and discuss it further! (Teacher 3)

Collaboration with the university researchers

The second way of talking about collaboration was in relation to the university researchers. The teachers emphasised collaboration in this sense as being part of something important, both for them but also for the research being done.

> It is a good occasion when you as a preschool teacher may collaborate and give [the researcher] materials that you need in your research. Similarly, we get the red thread [a Swedish expression for continuity] and insights into your great and wide work that develops and improves you, us and early childhood education. (Teacher 4)

The teacher teams appreciated the time spent together with the university researchers and felt they were of importance for the research being conducted, but also that this collaboration helped them to think further and be able to ask critical questions within the team about their work. They also saw it as a chance to learn more about the research field by meeting the university researchers in a general conversation. One of the teachers said, 'we need to update ourselves'. The value of collaboration with the university researchers expressed by the teacher teams in the survey will continue in the next category, in which the benefits and consequences of collaborative action research are presented.

Benefits and consequences

Incorporating the five analytical steps during one semester to work jointly with the mind map method meant there was time for the teachers to meet in between sessions and in staff meetings held for the purpose of planning their everyday work, and to reflect on the project. Three of the teachers in particular mentioned in the survey how they were influenced and how it was also transformed into other activities. They mentioned how they went back to the strengths and weaknesses shown in the mind map, and used these in further discussions within the team. Two of the practitioners made this explicit in the following quotes:

> mostly I think it was because it was easier for me to push various questions by referring to our mind maps and say, we've actually said that this is the way we do it and then we do it. It was also nice to have worked together with you in mind – what can we do now – how should we think about it here and so on. And it was commented on in our own planning. (Teacher 2)

> It has provided a secure foundation ... a sort of confirmation of how we work at our preschool and what we do when it is not working. (Teacher 3)

One question in the survey asked if they had used the same methods in their own work after the research project finished. No one explicitly said they had. Many of them admitted though that the mind map method was physically visible in their own units, hanging on the wall or having a place among other papers used for planning the daily work. It is a method that many teachers said can and should be used when planning their work. One of the practitioners talked about how they used mind maps in the team when they brainstormed new themes, both when planning the work with the children and when planning other activities, as Teacher 3 explains:

> Yes, type of a mind map (but with Post-It ...) when we brainstorm about new development areas, while planning the theme and when I as a mentor give suggestions on how to find a common subject for the development ... Very useful! Even with the kids when we vote for the activities or the purchase or selection of a movie ... (Teacher 3)

From the survey the teachers seemed to be very satisfied with their collaboration in the action research project, which gave them not just knowledge and insights into their work by visualising it, and deeper insights into research during the discussions, but also a tool, new to them, to use in their own work when planning activities for the children as practitioner researchers.

Discussion

In this chapter the purpose was to present a mind map method and to investigate by means of a survey how the teachers involved valued such participation. The findings gave insights into what the teachers say about their practices and also how their practices can be mapped out in a visualised picture of their professional learning and leadership (Rönnerman and Olin, 2012). Furthermore, the process of collaboration during the study made the teachers aware of how complex their work was, and the mind map method helped them to sort and choose topics for improvement, topics grounded in their own practice. The teacher teams also realised that the mind maps included more aspects to their work than just the actual work with the children. One such topic was participation with other parties (parents, special education teachers) and how their practice was influenced by policies in many more situations than they were aware of. This insight had an impact on teachers' future work on what topics to choose for further development. The research study shows how this method of collecting data and at the same time including the practitioners in the process has been beneficial. It gave the opportunity to delve deeper into what the practitioners were saying and thinking about their work. With the collaborative approach, the practitioners have been able to reflect on their discussions both with one another and with the university researcher, as the teams were kept together during the meetings and dialogue was emphasised. The use of both theory and proven experience became natural in these discussions and can be connected to professional learning and considered in terms of a PLC – a community with the purpose of critically investigating its environment with the aim of developing it to promote a child's learning and development, but not to judge the individual child's performance, as per the Swedish Education Act (Education Act, 2011).

Two important aspects of the dialogue were emphasised: 'listening' and 'giving responses' to one another. During the conversations the teachers were able to ask questions repeatedly so as to understand the meaning of what was discussed. By giving responses to one another, the teachers talked about how their team was strengthened and how they felt even more secure when they were able to develop this knowledge further in a dialogue with the university researchers, leading to a deeper understanding. Such meetings, based on dialogues, are important in conducting practitioner research and include seeking new knowledge to share collectively in the collaboration, as emphasised in a PLC (Nehring and Fitzsimmons, 2011). Likewise, the approach responds to collaborative action research based on the Nordic tradition (Salo and Rönnerman, 2014).

Because teachers had both an image in mind and a visualisation about their work the teachers pointed at how diffuse ideas turned into a clear articulation of their practice. It seemed as if the work itself became more visible, it was more alive in their minds. Moreover, it affected further discussions when the practitioners related to the mind map when discussing new themes or improvements. The practitioners were not just looking at a picture about their work; they were actually using the method themselves in constructing the picture. Their increased knowledge was afterwards used in planning and development.

Letting practitioners meet in their teams and first sketching a mind map of their practices in order to identify specific areas for inquiries has developed as a valued method in practitioner research among early childhood teachers (Nylund et al., 2010).

Conclusions and insights gained

In this last part I present three conclusions from the action research project and its values. Firstly, the teacher teams taking part in a collaborative action research project need to actively participate in order to develop their own learning. The use of a method should not just be presented to the practitioners, they have to be involved in the process of using the method in order to be able to transfer it to their own practice. Secondly, collective knowledge is achieved and can be compared to a professional learning community when teacher teams from several units in early childhood education participate in the same research project, in which knowledge is deepened, shared and constructed in a democratic dialogue. The teachers involved were strengthened both as individuals and as a collective (team). Thirdly, by being able to use a method that visualises a practice and labels its different parts, the practice becomes real and continues to be developed in a systematic way in aiming for higher quality for children's learning and development. By using the mind map collectively, the teacher team can develop a dialogue about their work but also develop an understanding about their practice.

Ongoing research considerations

- How could you employ the mind-mapping technique to investigate your work in your own workplace?
- Could collaborative action research be used in your workplace to investigate and improve something that has been worrying you for some time?

References

Education Act (2011) Den nya skollagen. Retrieved from: www.riksdagen.se/sv/ Dokument-Lagar/Lagar/Svenskforfattningssamling/Skollag-2010800_sfs-2010-800/ (last accessed 21 July 2014).

Edwards-Groves, C. and Rönnerman, K. (2013) 'Generating leading practices through professional learning', *Professional Development in Education*, 39 (1): 122–40.

Enö, M. (2005) *Att våga flyga: ett deltagarorienterat projekt om samtalets poten-tial och förskolepersonals konstruktion av det profesionella subjektet* [Dare to fly: collaborative project about the dialogue's potential for early child-hood education teachers' construction of the professional subject] (Diss).

Malmö Studies in Educational Sciences, Vol 19. Malmö: Malmö högskola, Lärarutbildningen.

Furu, E. M. and Lund, T. (2014) 'Development teams as translators of school reform ideas', in K. Rönnerman and P. Salo (eds), *Lost in Practice: Transforming Nordic Educational Action Research*. Rotterdam: Sense Publishers, pp. 153–70.

Gannerud, E. and Rönnerman, K. (2005) 'Studying teachers' work through mind-maps', *New Zealand Journal of Teachers' Work*, 2 (2): 76–82.

Groundwater-Smith, S., Mitchell, J., Mockler, N., Ponte, P. and Rönnerman, K. (2012) *Facilitating Practitioner Research: Developing Transformational Partnerships*. London: Routledge.

Gustavsen, B. (2001) 'Theory and practice: the mediating discourse', in P. Reason and H. Bradbury (eds), *Handbook of Action Research: Participative Inquiry and Practice*. London: Sage, pp. 17–26.

Hattie, J. (2011) *Visible Learning for Teachers*. London: Routledge.

Holmer, J. (1993) 'Deltagarorienterad forskning och forskarstödda läroprocesser' [Participatory research and research supported learning], in J. Holmer and B. Starrin (eds), *Deltagarorienterad forskning* [Participatory research]. Lund: Studentlitteratur, pp. 139–60.

Holmstrand, L. and Härnsten, G. (2003) *Förutsättningar för forskningscirklar i skolan: En kritisk granskning* [Prerequisites for research circles in school: a critical review] (Vol. 10). Stockholm: Myndigheten för Skolutveckling.

Kvale, S. (1998) *Den kvalitativa forskningsintervjun* [The qualitative research interview]. Lund: Studentlitteratur.

Larsson, S. and Nordvall, H. (2010) *Study Circles in Sweden: An Overview with a Bibliography of International Literature*. Mimer – The Swedish National Programme for Research on Popular Education. Linköping, Sweden: Linköping University Electronic Press.

Lund, T. (2008) 'Action research through dialogue conferences', in K. Rönnerman, E. M. Furu and P. Salo (eds), *Nurturing Praxis: Action Research in Partnerships between School and University in a Nordic Light*. Rotterdam: Sense Publishers, pp. 157–74.

McLaughlin, M. W. and Talbert, J. E. (2006) *Building School-Based Teacher Learning Communities*. New York: Teacher College Press.

Nehring, J. and Fitzsimmons, G. (2011) 'The professional learning community as subversive activity: countering the culture of conventional schooling', *Professional Development in Education*, 37 (4): 513–37.

Noffke, S. and Somekh, B. (2009) *The Sage Handbook of Educational Action Research*. London: Sage.

Nylund, M., Sandback, C., Wilhelmsson, B. and Rönnerman, K. (2010) *Aktionsforskning i förskolan: trots att schemat är fullt* [Action research in early childhood education]. Stockholm: Lärarförbundets förlag.

Reason, P. and Bradbury, H. (2001) (eds) *Handbook of Action Research: Participative Inquiry and Practice*. London: Sage.

Rönnerman, K. (2008) 'Empowering teachers: action research in partnership between school and university', in K. Rönnerman, E. M. Furu and P. Salo (eds),

Nurturing Praxis: Action Research in Partnerships between School and University in a Nordic Light. Rotterdam: Sense Publishers, pp. 157–74.

Rönnerman, K. (2011) 'Aktionsforskning – kunskapsproduktion i praktiken' [Action research – knowledge production in practice]. *Forskning om undervisning och lärande No 5,* [GM1], 51–62.

Rönnerman, K. and Olin, A. (2012) 'Kvalitetsarbete i förskolan belyst genom tre ledningsnivåer' [Quality work in pre-schools on three levels], *Pedagogisk forskning i Sverige,* 18 (3–4): 175–96.

Rönnerman, K. and Olin, A. (2014) 'Research circles: constructing a space for elaborating on being a teacher leader in preschools', in K. Rönnerman and P. Salo (eds), *Lost in Practice: Transforming Nordic Educational Action Research.* Rotterdam: Sense Publishers: 95–112.

Rönnerman, K. and Salo, P. (2012) '"Collaborative and action research" within education: a Nordic perspective', *Nordic Studies in Education,* 32 (1): 1–16.

Rönnerman, K. and Salo, P. (eds) (2014) *Lost in Practice: Transforming Nordic Educational Action Research.* Rotterdam: Sense Publishers.

Rönnerman, K., Salo, P. and Furu, E. M. (2008) 'Action research in the Nordic countries: a way to see possibilities', in K. Rönnerman, E. M. Furu and P. Salo (eds), *Nurturing Praxis: Action Research in Partnerships Between School and University in a Nordic Light.* Rotterdam: Sense Publishers, pp. 21–37.

Salo, P. and Rönnerman, K. (2014) 'The Nordic tradition of educational action research: in the light of practice architectures', in K. Rönnerman and P. Salo (eds), *Lost in Practice: Transforming Nordic Educational Action Research.* Rotterdam: Sense Publishers: 52–74.

Skolinspektionen (2012) *Förskola, före skola – lärande och bärande. Kvalitetsg ranskningsrapport om förskolans arbete med det förstärkta pedagogiska uppdraget* [Preschool, before school – learning and bearing. Quality report about work in preschools with the enhanced educational mission]. Retrieved from: www.skolinspektionen.se/ (last accessed 21 July 2014).

Skolverket (2011) Statistics. Retrieved from: www.skolverket.se/statistik-och-utvardering/statistik-i-tabeller/forskola/barn-och-grupper (last accessed 21 January 2014).

Skolverket (2014) *Curriculum for the Preschool Lpfö 98 revised 2010.* Retrieved from: www.skolverket.se/om-skolverket/publikationer/visa-enskild-publikation?_xurl_=http%3A%2F%2Fwww5.skolverket.se%2Fwtpub%2Fws%2Fskolbok%2Fwpubext%2Ftrycksak%2FRecord%3Fk%3D2704 (last accessed 8 December 2014).

Stoll, L., Bolam, R., McMahon, A., Wallace, M. and Thomas, S. (2006) 'Professional learning communities: a review of the literature', *Journal of Educational Change,* 7: 221–58.

Timperley, H. (2011) *Realizing the Power of Professional Learning.* Berkshire: Open University Press.

Wenger, E. (1998) *Communities of Practice: Learning, Meaning and Identity.* Cambridge: Cambridge University Press.

6

RECONCEPTUALISING SERVICES FOR YOUNG CHILDREN THROUGH DIALOGUE IN A SOUTH AFRICAN VILLAGE

Norma Rudolph and Mary James

Key words   South Africa; dialogue; democratic decision-making and action; early childhood development; action research; participatory decision-making and action; child rights; appreciative inquiry; action learning.

Chapter overview

This chapter explores the use of a critical participatory capacity building approach that was developed and trialled in a complex multi-phased action research project in South Africa. The eight-year project was led by the Children's Institute at the University of Cape Town, but was conducted in collaboration with many partners and contained multiple streams of learning and action. The research project was called Caring Schools and its primary purpose was to reconceptualise services for children in the context of the AIDS pandemic and legacy of apartheid. The co-authored chapter is based on one research team's story about their participatory journey in using an appreciative enquiry approach, research process documents, and a

(Continued)

(Continued)

final reflective conversation between the two co-authors, four years after the partnership ended. The chapter discusses aspects of action learning used to promote democratic decision-making and action in early childhood education at the village level. The co-authors are the director of a service provider organisation, Little Elephant Training Centre for Early Education (LETCEE) and the principal researcher from the Children's Institute. The key themes addressed are appreciative participatory processes for reconceptualising children's services to focus on child wellbeing through democratic decision-making and action. In the chapter readers can see how dialogue is used to promote social transformation through acknowledging and supporting agency with children and adults.

Rationale for study and how the authors came to be working together

The main focus of the eight-year Caring Schools study was investigating an expanded role of schools to support the growing numbers of children in difficult circumstances. However, during the initial phase, it became clear that by focusing only on those children already attending school many of the children in most need would be excluded, including young children and older out-of-school children. In addition to schools, early childhood services offered another potential entry point and gateway for services. Consequently, LETCEE was invited to participate as one of four partners testing the capacity building approach in one component of the second phase of the study. LETCEE was selected as it was implementing a family-based approach to early childhood development (ECD) rather than only focusing on centre-based services. This chapter explores the use of the critical participatory capacity building approach by LETCEE.

The site of learning and action

Mbuba is a small community in a mountainous area of the Kwa-Zulu Natal province in South Africa. The homes, mostly made in traditional Zulu style with wattle and daub, are scattered over a wide area and most roads are gravel. Few homes have electricity or running water and there are no flushing toilets. There are few services in this remote rural area.

Community health workers provide some primary health care, and a mobile clinic visits once a month when weather and other contingencies allow. There is no public transport system and the private taxi service is poor and unreliable. According to the 2001 census, about half of the approximately 10,000 residents in the ward were children under the age of 17. Only 25 per cent of the economically active population (between the ages of 15 and 65) were employed. Almost 25 per cent of households had no cash income, another 50 per cent had less than approximately $2000 and only about 11 per cent had more than $2000 annual income. Many men were absent, working in cities around South Africa. Some women were employed as labourers on the surrounding farms (Statistics South Africa, n.d.).

Mbuba constitutes one ward, which is the smallest unit in the system of local governance in South Africa, and has one elected representative on the local municipal council. Traditional leadership also plays an important role in the management and control of the area.

In many homes, a grandmother or elderly relative takes care of the children. The three preschools in the area are inaccessible for most children as the walking distance is too far or the fees too costly. Enrolment and attendance at two under-resourced primary schools is relatively good, despite some children having to walk up to 5–6 kilometres, sometimes alone, to get to the nearest school. Some children as young as four years old could walk up to 2 kilometres. The proportion of high school children enrolled is far lower than for primary school. There is no high school in the area and all children have to catch a taxi or walk the 5 kilometres to the next community to attend school. Basic education is compulsory in grades 1–9, or for children aged 7–15. In addition to financial constraints, enrolment and attendance is hampered by family commitments such as child minding and household chores and perceived failures of the education system.

The following sections describe the context, rationale and methodology of the larger Caring Schools study.

Rethinking service provisioning

Many children in South Africa live in extremely difficult circumstances in the wake of apartheid and the AIDS pandemic. In response to these challenges, the Caring Schools action research project was initiated in 2005, by the Children's Institute in partnership with the largest South African teacher's union (SADTU) to investigate an expanded role for schools as gateways for service provision and support. Extensive research and consultation had documented the impact of AIDS on households (especially children) and on service providers such as educators (Giese et al., 2003, 2004). Given the scale and complexity of challenges, it was necessary to think beyond the obvious functions of children's services and to maximise contact opportunities with children needing help. While the main focus of the larger project was on the role of schools, the LETCEE partnership provided an opportunity to include services for young children.

Methodology: appreciative systemic action research

The learning and change strategy incorporated into the project has its roots in the first author's (Norma) experiential learning with communities in different contexts using critical pedagogy (Freire, 1970; Giroux, 1997). In particular it draws on the power of dialogue to transform relationships, build community and drive social change (Freire, 1970). Drawing on variants of action research in a process oriented methodology, elements of systemic action research are used to create streams of parallel and interlocking inquiry synthesised with an appreciative orientation and fuelled by the emancipatory and democratic commitments of participant-driven collective critical inquiry to achieve momentum.

Action research is understood as a 'hub for a mixture of methods' in which narrative is a core process (Burns, 2007: 133). According to Carr and Kemmis (1986), three conditions are necessary and sufficient for action research:

> Firstly, a project takes as its subject matter a social practice, regarding it as a form of strategic action susceptible of improvement; secondly, the project proceeds through a spiral of cycles of planning, acting, observing and reflecting, with each of these activities being systematically and self-critically implemented and interrelated; thirdly the project involves those responsible for the practice in each of the moments of the activity, widening participation in the project gradually to include others affected by the practice, and maintaining collaborative control over the process (Carr and Kemmis, 1986: 165–6).

In terms of Hart and Bond's (1995) continuum from the 'experimental', through the 'organisational' and the 'professionalising' to the 'empowering', this research took a radical and empowering approach to learning and social change. It used many of the features of 'critical participatory action research' discussed by Kemmis et al. (2014). In particular, the design and implementation gave careful attention to the 'kinds of relationships that need to be developed among participants, institutions and other stakeholders' in order to generate communicative space and action that is voluntary and inclusive (Kemmis et al., 2014: 33). The approach brought people together to reflect and act on social and educational practices in disciplined ways (Kemmis et al., 2014).

Strategies that privilege communication to engage participants in collaborative action for change towards social justice were selected. The approach is best summed up by Burns' (2007) description of 'systemic action research' as a 'process through which communities and organisations can adapt and respond purposefully to their constantly changing environments (Burns, 2007: 1). It supports participative solutions to entrenched problems and enables groups to work with uncertainty. This could be referred to as 'participatory learning and action' (PLA) and follows the fundamental principles set out by Bergold and Thomas (2012). There is a strong connection between democracy and the research as the primary aim is democratic decision-making and action. An inclusive 'safe space' is generated to facilitate communication and encourage the revelation and discussion of different perspectives and opinions. A 'snowball system' is designed to include more and more participants in the conversation based on the understanding that there will be different degrees of participation. The aim is both to increase the number of participants and strengthen the nature of participation (Bergold and Thomas, 2012).

However, it differs from most action research in that instead of using a problem-solving approach, it uses an explicitly appreciative approach that builds on strengths. Appreciative inquiry (Elliott, 1999; Watkins et al., 2011) was used to both involve as wide a range of role-players as feasible in the conversation about child wellbeing, and to generate energy for action by starting with reflection on what people already do well and know how to do, rather than using the more common practice of participatory approaches that start with identifying a problem. An action oriented rights-based approach (Rudolph et al., 2008; Ward, 2008) was used to raise consciousness and mobilise action to protect child rights and support wellbeing of children, families and communities.

Systemic action research 'offers a learning architecture' for a change process of 'in-depth inquiry, multi-stakeholder analysis, experiential action and experiential learning' (Burns, 2007: 1). It has the potential to be 'built into the "everyday" practice of community activists, professional policymakers and change agents (as well as students and researcher) rather than a specialist process for an expert researcher' (Burns 2007: 4). Systemic action research has the potential to affect transformational change as it offers 'an embedded learning process through which policy and practice can be constructed on the ground' (Burns 2007: 4).

Our adaptation could be referred to as 'appreciative systemic action research', with the understanding that the participatory and critical features are implied. This is a political process that, when successful, necessarily involves shifting the balance of power in a variety of different immediate relationships and addressing the structural barriers to the protection of child rights.

Description of study

Underlying assumptions

Given the growing numbers of children in difficulties in South Africa, our primary assumption is that the wellbeing of all children requires systemic and structural change at all levels, from the individual, the family, communities, through to social institutions such as schools, clinics, faith-based organisations and community structures. Different constructions of childhood, families and societies must be explored in order to agree on strategies to support optimal wellbeing of children, their families and communities. All spheres of government – vertically, from local to national, and horizontally, across all relevant government ministries and departments, particularly education, health and social welfare – are involved. Such change necessarily requires significant shifts in understanding and beliefs as well as consensus building. There is consequently no 'quick fix' solution.

Aims

The aim of this appreciative systemic action research initiative was to reconceptualise provisioning for children in the context of the AIDS pandemic in South Africa. The intention was to investigate how public provision for children might be reconceptualised as 'ethical and political endeavours that require explicit choices about who we think children are, what is good childhood and the purpose of public provision for children' (Moss and Petrie, 2002: 2). Given the impact of the AIDS pandemic and the range of barriers to learning and development, the challenge of an uncertain future called for engaging a wide range of individuals and sectors in collaborative action based on dialogue in the 'social arena rather than essential truths revealed through science' (Moss and Petrie, 2002: 2). In terms of Moss and Petrie (2002), the investigation was about how schools (and other forms of provision) as sites for 'democratic and ethical practice involving critical thinking, might contribute to the political project of influencing the direction change takes' (Moss and Petrie, 2002: 2). The primary focus was on the possibility of 'creating relationships and solidarities between children, between adults and between adults and children' (Moss and Petrie, 2002: 2). This involved a shift from notion of provision as primarily 'technical and disciplinary undertakings, concerned with regulation, surveillance and normalisation, instrumental in rationality and purpose' (Moss and Petrie, 2002: 2).

The capacity building approach

The action research process had two main phases. In the first phase a capacity building approach was developed in four school communities and documented in a handbook (see Rudolph et al., 2008). The capacity building approach provides many activities to engage a variety of different role-players in the conversation and action to promote child wellbeing. The key activity is the 'Journey of Hope' (Rudolph et al., 2008), which introduces the notion of a continuum between wellbeing and vulnerability and provides an opportunity to engage with different constructions of childhoods, build a shared vision of a better future for children, start making commitments and taking small steps towards realising that dream. It was designed in such a way that it can be rolled out in a park or other public space to engage passers-by in the conversation and then invite them into the action research process. To begin, participants generate fictitious stories about children. They then place each child on the continuum between wellbeing and vulnerability and discuss possible risk and protective factors that could move the child in either direction along the continuum. In the context of AIDS this activity provides an important opportunity to hold public conversations about these complex issues while protecting confidentiality of real children in the community. Through dialogue in groups about the potential risk and protective factors that might impact on children, a collaborative process of consensus building is generated. Different perspectives are presented and negotiated. In particular, participants engage with protective factors and make the links to rights.

In the next stage participants imagine a better future for children in the community and prioritise action through identifying specific dreams that are organised into three groups: those that can be translated into action without any additional help or resources from outside the group; those that will need a lot of resources and help; and the rest that fall in the middle. It is then possible to start taking action individually or in small groups to start realising the dreams. At regular intervals the groups meet to reflect on progress and plan the next phase of action. Each cycle starts with identifying what is going well and the successes, however small, from the previous cycle can be celebrated to generate energy to take on more challenging actions that might need to be broken into smaller steps. In this way participants are generating and managing the data about their journeys towards a better future. In some cases the data from different groups is collated and presented to a bigger group or a number of small groups.

These appreciative inquiry cycles also provide important opportunities for large numbers of people to engage in the same conversation without being in the same room at the same time. A key assumption is that data is generated and used to present multiple possibilities and perspectives among multiple people, all of whose points of view are considered legitimate versions of reality. For example, while parents and school management might assume that the school is safe, children often present a very different reality. The emphasis is on reaching new social agreements and mindsets that can generate new realities through future actions. Sometimes, the action required can be as simple as cutting long grass or ensuring an adult is always available to keep children safe when they go to the toilet. Success with these small changes can motivate efforts to take on greater challenges.

While each local co-research team is responsible for initiating the process in one geographic area, it is essential that they do not collect and analyse the research themselves, but involve as wide a group as possible. Collective inquiry is the key difference between traditional and action research.

> The creation and development of distributed leadership is an essential part of large system action research. It is not only a positive by-product but a crucial element in the development of the networks that drive the process. Effective action inquiry is based on relationship building that is in turn built on trust building. Leaders that emerge from the process will be able to open doors that no external facilitator will be able to open. (Burns 2007: 101)

Shifting from individual to collective inquiry is no easy task, as we discovered through our learning journey in Mbuba.

Testing and strengthening the capacity development approach

The main focus of the second phase of the action research project, in which LETCEE participated, was to test and strengthen the capacity building approach developed in the first phase. Four co-research teams with no experience of action research each used the approach over two years in the one site in which they were already operating in different parts of South Africa. Each local co-research team included one team leader, responsible for communication between the team and the principal researcher at the Children's Institute (Norma). Broad guidelines were provided for the composition of each team, with circumstances determining the membership in each case. The LETCEE core team was led by the LETCEE Director (Mary), with a community projects manager and two community facilitators responsible for field-work. The team worked closely with the traditional leadership of the village, other LETCEE project field staff, residents of the village and service providers, such as school staff, social workers and health professionals. Children and young people participated, not only as recipients of support but as change agents.

The Children's Institute facilitated a process through which teams met at six-month intervals in national meetings to reflect on the developments in the previous period and plan for the next. Between these meetings each team implemented the process in their own geographic area and the principal researcher communicated with team leaders through telephone, email and in some cases face-to-face meetings during field visits to the site. Partner team reports on the process in the previous period informed the agenda for the national meetings.

Learning and action with LETCEE

The partnership was timely in terms of LETCEE's development from a preschool established in 1991 to a 'training'[1] organisation playing a leading role in the development and implementation of a comprehensive approach to ECD. Peter Rule (2005) describes LETCEE as 'a unique organisation with its own contextually specific history, as a microcosm of the evolving ECD field'. In particular, he draws attention to how the organisation has been 'shaped on the one hand by the increasing formalization and regulation of the field, and its evolving understanding of ECD as a part of community development, on the other' (Rule, 2005: 121). The partnership offered by the Children's Institute aligned with LETCEE's understanding of the 'centrality of community involvement to the success of ECD initiatives' (Rule, 2005: 128). LETCEE had started to train family facilitators to provide home-based early childhood services for young children unable to attend preschools on account of family illness or poverty in the context of the

---

[1] The term 'training' is used in South Africa to refer to various forms of capacity building and development of teachers and early childhood practitioners, including short courses and full qualifications.

AIDS pandemic. This work was extended to helping families access a range of government services, including birth certificates and cash transfers. At the start of the partnership, LETCEE was already a learning organisation and the goals and values of LETCEE aligned strongly with those of the research.

Overview of transformation

In the process of writing this chapter, as co-authors, we held a reflexive conversation about the action research partnership four years after it ended. In this part of the chapter, for the sake of clarity, we refer to ourselves by name and use dialogue form. Here is an excerpt from the conversation.

Mary: LETCEE regards the action research partnership as empowering, especially in the way it helped us recognise the value of our work.

Norma: In any partnership, I think the balance of power is important and collaboration involves building on each other's ideas and energy. Scaffolding each other and building on strengths.

Mary: We appreciated the principles that guided our action research partnership, in the way we were consulted and able to contribute to the research design. This contrasted with our frequent experience of being instructed rather than being consulted by partners. The partnership was particularly helpful in building capacity of the co-research team, who liked being valued and having their opinions taken seriously. Their horizons were widened and they changed their perceptions of LETCEE being a small, localised entity to fitting into a bigger world. In particular our skills in collecting data and documenting our work were strengthened.

Norma: What were some of your lessons?

Mary: Our most important lesson was recognising that everybody has valuable experience to contribute, including children and people with low levels of literacy. Parents have realised they have rights and can question teachers and authorities. They are starting to overcome their feelings of inadequacy and regarding themselves as less than people with status. For example, previously, there was a disjuncture between home and school, but families are confident to engage with schools, ask questions and explain to teachers the need for young children to play and be active instead of merely spending hours in repetitious recitation. Families are no longer onlookers but equal partners and when teachers are consistently absent parents go to school to say they are not happy.

Norma: That is a very important achievement and heartening that families are taking their power and protecting their children's rights. Our readers might not realise, firstly, that teacher absenteeism is very high in the context of AIDS and, secondly, there is no system or funding to regularly replace absent teachers.

Mary: The capacity building strategy has influenced the way LETCEE is guided by the communities we serve. We encourage everyone to tell their stories, discuss priorities and start taking collaborative action. We allocate time for listening to families and communities before we get to the business of doing. We recognise families as experts who know the priorities for their children and that community. Now we talk to different groups, not only the community leaders and those who are most articulate. We hold community conversations in different places, including taxis and taverns to engage men where they go to drink and the places where youth gather.

Helpful strategies

Norma: What would you say are the most helpful capacity building strategies or approaches you learned though our partnership?

Mary: Appreciative inquiry! LETCEE uses an appreciative approach all the time now both with communities and within the organisation. For example, the ECD home visitors are asked to report on at least one good news story each month. They report on 'moments of success' that are used to illustrate possible solutions to common challenges. The same approach is used in meetings with caregivers.

Norma: Could you explain how you are using any other helpful ideas you learned?

Mary: Yes. The notion of 'champion' has helped us deal with the tendency of some 'bossy' people to control and exclude others. We explain that a real 'champion' motivates others to become champions for children and welcomes everyone to participate and work together. The 'community analysis' activity helps the community committee decide whom to 'inform', to 'consult' or 'involve' depending on the activity and the levels of influence and interest of different people. By continually informing everyone (even those with low interest), eventually they might get involved. Most actions can be taken without asking advice or permission, but it is important to know which officials to consult before certain actions are taken. Initially LETCEE only involved people with high influence in the community, but now we realise that anyone interested can participate and with time also gain influence.

Norma: That is interesting. Inclusive strategies clearly promote democratic decision-making. Are there any activities you have adapted?

Mary: Oh, yes, remember the community mapping strategy where you suggested we ask groups to map their community! LETCEE has recently begun using Google Earth with community groups. We project the area onto a screen, identify a well-known landmark, and then using street view (or tipping the picture so it's like a street view), use the mouse to 'walk' along the roads and paths. Each person talks about her/his favourite places and they mark the 'good', 'helpful' or 'safe' places in the community. These may be homes, or more public places. We then do the same thing marking places where children might feel safe, protected or welcome. They identify places that are not helpful or safe and discuss strategies for making changes. Through mapping, they also identify and evaluate service provisioning and use the data to plan the appointment of additional ECD home visitors.

Norma: What an excellent idea! I would never have thought of using that kind of technology in a village where few homes have electricity.

Challenges

Norma: OK, we have spoken about the successes, what about the challenges?

Mary: Time was a big challenge.

Norma: Of course, the pressure of time was the greatest challenge in all components of the research. There was a major tension between research funding constraints and time needed to bring about meaningful change in communities. I know this was an especially big problem for LETCEE, as you agreed to take on the additional demands of the action research process alongside their already demanding programme activities without any additional funding. What else?

Mary: At first the community was suspicious about the intentions of the partnership. For many years outsiders have come into the community and made promises and raised expectations that had not been realised.

Norma: That happens so often when external 'experts' think they know best.

Mary: Sometimes in national meetings, it was difficult for LETCEE to see how we fitted into the bigger action research process, as we were the only partner focusing primarily on young children and using the community rather than the school as an entry-point.

Norma: I understand, but from the overall research perspective LETCEE made a very important contribution to widening the perspective of the other partners whose primary focus was children already in formal schooling. Can we focus now on the learning process?

Reflecting on the learning process

Mary: Some of the activities asked community members to imagine a better future for their children, but I think that 'imagination' is not a huge part of the reality of hard everyday life of people in Mbuba. Using 'metaphor' and the idea of travelling into the future is quite abstract and caused some problems in communities burdened by the daily struggle for survival.

Norma: Interesting! Let's reflect a bit more about this. What activity shall we use to focus the discussion?

Mary: What about the Busometer activity?

Norma: Great! Let's start by describing the Busometer activity to our readers and then reflect on some reports on how it was used by LETCEE facilitators.

Description of the Busometer activity

The Busometer activity is designed to focus reflection as part of the on-going participatory process to build a 'caring community'. The metaphor of a 'journey' is used to describe the collaborative decision-making and action process. It works best when the community has already started discussion and action to build a caring community. The idea is to use a bus or any other relevant form of transport to represent the vehicle supporting the collaborative journey. Starting with each participant considering her or his own role in the process, different fictitious role-players and groups are identified and their participation is discussed using questions such as the following:

- What is my contribution?
- Who is driving the bus at the present moment?
- Who is reading the map and helping the driver with directions?
- Who are the noisy passengers?
- Who is sitting at the back?
- Who is just coming along for the ride?
- Who has not noticed that the bus has got to get somewhere at a certain time?
- Who maintains and services the bus?
- What is helping the bus move forward?
- Is there anything that slows the bus down?
- Who is still waiting at the bus stop?
- Who can't get to the bus stop?
- Who has not even heard of the bus?

Layered learning in the direction of transformation

In the report we selected to focus our reflection, the facilitator uses the Busometer activity as the introductory activity with 65 grade-five primary school children. The process that unfolded was very different from the intention described above. While the children provided some insights into the way they perceive the community, some of their responses suggested that they were saying what children think adults expect from them.

Here is an extract from Mary and Norma's reflection on the report.

Norma: What is your first impression when you read the facilitator report?

Mary: It illustrates the problem I mentioned about using 'metaphor'.

Norma: The report generated different questions and learnings for me, such as: how might activities be understood and used differently? Why are activities used differently? What learning arises from the different ways the activity is used? What are the different constructions of childhood and society? What kind of reflection would be helpful at different levels of learning?

Mary: That is interesting, please give some more detail.

Norma: The children helped the facilitator learn as she reported, 'This workshop has taught me so many things, most of which

I didn't think were possible'. She has taken the important step of 'growing the conversation' and taking it into the primary school. Most importantly she is listening to children and is taking their perspectives seriously. We both know that would be very unusual in that kind of school with very large classes and the usual formal teacher-directed pedagogical practice.

Mary: Yes, she had planned to follow this activity with a mapping activity, in which participants draw the community and mark the helpful or safe places and unsafe or unhelpful places, but had not managed to do both in the two hours available. In retrospect, it might have been better to start with the mapping activity in terms of the purposes for which each activity had been designed.

Norma: Yes. This shows that there are no right or wrong ways to use the activities. It is the reflection that is important, so that we can keep learning and moving in the right direction.

Mary: Yes. Through presenting the perspectives of children to the adults an important initial step was taken towards helping adults understand the importance of listening to children. The dominant view in this community has been, 'Children should be seen and not heard'.

Norma: So the activity generated many levels of learning: for the children, the facilitator, the co-research team, the committee and community. We need to make sure that nothing anyone does causes harm and that the change is towards social justice.

Mary: Can you think of some specific examples of change that emerged from adults listening to children?

Norma: The community organised a roster of adults to supervise when children reported they did not feel safe in the children's park. Also, the community stopped traditional leaders using corporal punishment on children and through the dialogue a much better general understanding of early childhood issues was generated.

Mary: The overall intention of the action research process was to build a shared understanding of a better future and start working towards it. I agree that there might be a sense of hopelessness in many communities in South Africa but it is possible to generate hope through taking small experimental steps towards the kind of society that people would like and celebrating these small successes to generate the energy to make bigger changes.

Norma: Indeed! Mbuba has started on this journey. If we go back to the reports we were discussing earlier, the same facilitator had used both the mapping and Busometer activities in the previous week with the community committee and reported, 'After the activities it was easy for the committee to see what each person can do to change the community or to make it a better community'.

Mary: I don't think the problem is in using 'metaphor' but having opportunities and guidance to practise and develop facilitation capacity. Through the action research project we planned to develop a handbook that could be used in different contexts. However, we realised that it would be more difficult than anticipated. Language and levels of literacy are extremely challenging. We realised that developing reflective facilitators with sound questioning skills is the most important component of the approach. We explored blended approaches using face-to-face engagement with written materials in order to balance cost with support in the reflective process.

Conclusions and insights gained

The learning continues but it is not always easy to measure.

Mary noted that:

Through the reflection and writing this chapter, I realised just how much the partnership and capacity building approach has improved what we do. It is not easy to notice when and how we learn or easily link cause and effect. However, looking back I can see how the action research changed the way we work – from trying to solve problems for the community, to working in partnership with them. Community committees now co-manage projects as partners, not just beneficiaries.

Some readers might be expecting test scores and scientific measurements of progress, but this is a story of people in extremely difficult circumstances slowly claiming agency and taking small steps in the direction of the future they want for themselves and their children though inclusive participation and deliberative decision-making.

The experience in Mbuba confirms the general conclusion that the capacity building approach can build trust and mutual respect to support open and honest dialogue. An action oriented rights-based approach helps key role-players understand their rights, roles and duties in building a web of caring relationships and taking action to improve wellbeing through facilitating dialogue between rights claimants and duty-bearers. However, this work is complex, difficult and time-consuming. In communities with the largest number of children in difficult circumstances, community safety nets are threadbare and the services to which children are entitled are often absent or inaccessible. While appreciative systemic action research holds much promise, it requires a sufficient number of facilitators with the necessary skills and time to initiate and drive the process. Change is most easily achieved at the individual level, but much more difficult to achieve at larger institutional and societal levels.

Learning is continuing beyond the finite Caring Schools action research activity. LETCEE has contributed learnings and activities to the collaborative process to develop a model for a South African ECD home visiting programme. The idea of reconceptualising services for children through democratic decision-making and experimentation has been taken up and adapted by many organisations nationally and across the region, including through the programme of Care and Support for Teaching and Learning (CSTL) of the Southern African Development Community (SADC). The Children's Institute undertook a regional policy review and developed a CSTL framework for SADC. The capacity building approach is being used in an in service Teachers' Diploma in Psychosocial Care, Support and Protection being tested by the Regional Psycho-Social Support Forum (REPSSI) in Zambia and to be offered by teacher development institutions across Southern and East Africa.

Ongoing research considerations

- How could you use the revised capacity building approach in other locations?
- How could you adapt the capacity building approach to be offered through academic university programmes?

References

Bergold, J. and Thomas, S. (2012) 'Participatory research methods: a methodological approach in motion', *Historical Social Research*, 37 (4): 191–222.

Burns, D. (2007) *Systematic Action Research: A Strategy for Whole System Change*. Bristol: Policy.

Carr, W. and Kemmis, S. (1986) *Becoming Critical: Education, Knowledge and Action Research*. London: Falmer.

Elliott, C. (1999) *Locating the Energy for Change: An Introduction to Appreciative Inquiry*. Winnipeg: International Institute for Sustainable Development.

Freire, P. (1970) *Pedagogy of the Oppressed*. New York: Continuum.

Giese, S., Meintjes, H., Croke, R. and Chamberlain, R. (2003) *Health and Social Services to Address the Needs of Orphans and Other Vulnerable Children in the Context of HIV/AIDS: Research Report and Recommendations*. Pretoria: Children's Institute and National Department of Health.

Giese, S., Meintjes, H., Croke, R. and Chamberlain, R. (2004) 'Reaching vulnerable children: The role of schools as nodes of care and support in the context of HIV/AIDS', paper presented at the AIDS 2004 Conference, Bangkok, Thailand.

Giroux, H. A. (1997) *Pedagogy and the Politics of Hope: Theory, Culture, and Schooling – A Critical Reader*. Boulder, CO: Westview Press.

Hart, E. and Bond, M. (1995) *Action Research for Health and Social Care: A Guide to Practice*. Buckingham, PA: Open University Press.

Kemmis, S., McTaggart, R. and Nixon, R. (2014) 'A new view of participation: participation', *Public Spheres: The Action Research Planner*, 33–49. DOI: 10.1007/978-981-4560-67-2_2.

Moss, P. and Petrie, P. (2002) *From Children's Services to Children's Spaces: Public Policy, Children and Childhood*. London: RoutlegdgeFalmer.

Rudolph, N., Monson, J., Collett, K. and Sonn, B. (2008) *Champions for Children Handbook: How to Build a Caring School Community (Pilot Version)*. Capetown, SA: University of Capetown.

Rule, P. (2005) 'Ten years of early childhood development: a case study of Little Elephant Training Centre for Early Education', *Journal of Education*, 35: 121–38.

Statistics South Africa (n.d.) Umvoti municipality. Retrieved from: http://www.google.com.au/url?sa=t&rct=j&q=&esrc=s&source=web&cd=1&ved=0CB4QFjAA&url=http%3A%2F%2Fjoe.ukzn.ac.za%2FLibraries%2FNo_35_2005%2FTen_years_of_early_childhood_development_a_case_tudy_of_Little_Elephant_Training_Centre_for_Early_Education.sflb.ashx&ei=2JleVePgCMmD8gXmiYGoCg&usg=AFQjCNF51jT3pfEWcgCe3czT5_Linc7qAA&sig2=vPjcF1R-UmbbRSd5ByPdJg&bvm=bv.93990622,d.dGc&cad=rja (last accessed 22 May 2015).

Ward, P. (2008) *A Southern Africa Facilitators' Guide to Child Rights Programming Training*. Hatfield, South Africa: Save the Children Sweden.

Watkins, J. M., Mohr, B. J. and Kelly, R. (2011) *Appreciative Inquiry: Change at the Speed of Imagination* (Vol. 35): San Francisco, CA: Pfeiffer.

7

SUSTAINING CURRICULUM RENEWAL IN WESTERN SYDNEY: THREE PARTICIPANT VIEWS

Linda Newman, Janet Keegan
and Trish Heeley

Key words   practitioner research; reflexive methodology; early
childhood curriculum; pedagogical leadership.

Chapter overview

In this chapter, the authors reflect on their experiences of participating
in practitioner research, initially from their respective positions as
academic, manager and teacher, and subsequently on their shifting
roles as they became collaborative co-researchers in ongoing action
research. The chapter is written as a reflective boundary-crossing
conversation about their early experiences in an initial umbrella
participatory project which became known as the Jean Denton project
(Newman and Mowbray, 2012), comprised of five distinct practitioner
groups, and their later experiences within the ongoing Curriculum
Renewal Group (CRG), which was one of the five initial groups.

The chapter focuses on the CRG and also provides a brief outline of
the umbrella Jean Denton project to establish the context for the
origins of the CRG and subsequent discussion. The CRG was made up

(Continued)

(Continued)

of staff located within a large local government-based early childhood education organisation in Western Sydney, Australia, and focused on reconceptualising curriculum through action research cycles. Six years further on, the authors discuss how the project has grown, adapted and thrived to position the organisation at the forefront of national changes through a policy initiative aimed at pedagogical leadership and early childhood education quality. Reflecting on their engagement in the CRG, the authors consider the potential of universities to work in partnership with practitioners within the context of policy reform and issues of sustainability of these relationships. The discussion raises questions about emerging professional identities as practitioners become researchers, and academics become practitioner research participants, affording readers the opportunity to observe the journey undertaken by a practitioner and a manager whose daily work formerly didn't include research.

The chapter addresses the key themes of early childhood education curriculum; practitioner research; action research; reflexive methodology; communities of practice; collaborative research; and pedagogical leadership.

Readers of this chapter can expect to learn how a relatively small project can develop and spread across an organisation. They will read about the theoretical foundations underpinning one project, the practical realities, the challenges and the rewards of curriculum renewal through action research.

Rationale for study and how the authors came to be working together

The genesis of the CRG was in conversations over several years between the authors and others from local government children's services management as they reflected on their concerns about curriculum and pedagogical leadership. The authors were professionally connected through the local government provider organisation, in which Janet Keegan was the Children's Services Manager, Trish Heeley worked as a teacher/director of an early childhood centre and Linda Newman was an early childhood university academic as well as community board member of the Children's Services Cooperative Board. They each assumed different roles in providing leadership to early childhood educators from 23 children's centres in the organisation. Janet and Trish responded to Linda's invitation to join the Jean Denton practitioner research group and began the CRG as they planned, implemented and generated data from their first project in that group. When the Jean Denton project concluded, Janet and Trish chose to continue with the CRG, inviting Linda to join them as a collaborator, hence shifting her role from that of academic facilitator in other peoples' projects to a collaborating researcher within one of those projects. This project is now in its sixth year, though Linda left the project midway when moving to another city and university. This chapter provides the opportunity to reflect on achievements and insights gained.

When the Jean Denton project commenced, early CRG data showed that services were sending educators to a range of externally provided, one-off curriculum training sessions. The team recognised that participants were receiving inconsistent and contradictory information. This was resulting in educators frequently returning to their services unclear about the expectations for curriculum programming and documentation, lacking clarity about what was required, and wanting further guidance on curriculum implementation at the centre level. This reflects the research literature which shows that effective continuing professional development (CPD) should meet both individual teachers' and collective institutional needs. Early (2010) advocates a personalised approach in which teachers' knowledge and experience is considered because the more influence teachers have over their own learning, the more likely it is to be sustainable.

From Trish's perspective as a teacher director, there was a keen interest in investigating the way curriculum was practised at her centre. While some aspects of environments, routines and practices had moved to reflect an emergent curriculum model, considered contemporary practice at the time (Arthur et al., 2008; Jones and Nimmo, 1994), the documentation of programmes and assessment of children were still strongly framed by developmentally appropriate practice. At around this time Edwards (2007) documented the struggle for educators trained in developmental constructivist approaches, as Trish's team were, when they moved towards adoption of newer socioculturally informed approaches as represented in curriculum frameworks current at that time. This was an issue needing examination. In Trish's view, which was supported by research (Campbell, 2003), staff participation in one-off, isolated training sessions about the recently developed voluntary curriculum, called 'The Practice of Relationships, the NSW Curriculum Framework' (NSW Department of Community Services, 2001), had not had a lasting effect on practices and understandings. During performance planning and review meetings practitioners in Trish's centre raised their lack of confidence in implementing and documenting their work with children in correspondence with the framework.

From Janet's point of view, reflections by her management team about curriculum implementation across the organisation's 23 centres had identified a lack of consistency in implementation and apparent confusion about what should be done, who was responsible for implementation and how curriculum was to be evaluated and assessed. The management team wondered to what extent curriculum quality was dependent on the centre director's leadership, qualifications, knowledge and ongoing training, resulting in varying levels of quality in different settings. It was also clear from Janet's discussions with educators that the professional development they were attending was unhelpful, they were finding curriculum development and programming onerous and time consuming, with limited success in quality outcomes. This indicated that an alternative approach to staff development was required. In response, a socioculturally informed approach incorporating communities of learners was planned (Edwards, 2007; Lave and Wenger, 1991).

Aims of the project

During the initial Jean Denton project, Janet and Trish devised a series of aims for curriculum renewal that have remained ongoing in the life of the CRG. The ways to achieve these, and the participation of practitioners, have since been amended, reflecting the ongoing reflexive action research cycle process:

- to identify the current curriculum development understanding and capacities of educators
- to develop clear guidelines and documents to support educators to implement contemporary early childhood curriculum
- to design a contemporary curriculum renewal process that ensures educators receive effective training and support
- to engage an educator from each service in the CRG process in an effort to create a sense of pedagogical leadership that engages all educators
- to monitor and evaluate renewal processes and outcomes.

The project was guided by the research question: 'What happens to curriculum documentation when a participatory model of curriculum review is used to support reflexive practice in early childhood settings?'

Theoretical perspective

The CRG study was framed as a practitioner research project delivered through action research cycles. Here we define practitioner research in ways aligned to Cochran-Smith and Lytle's definition for teacher research – research that fits under the conceptual umbrella of practitioner inquiry, with its inherent stance that 'deep changes in practice can only be brought about by those closest to the day-to-day work of teaching and learning ... [and with the] potential for re-thinking, resisting, and re-forming the ways we think about, and take action regarding, the arrangements and purposes of [early childhood education]' (Cochran-Smith and Lytle, 2009: 39). We use the term practitioner research rather than their term teacher research as the project involved managers, teachers, an academic and educators with qualifications other than teaching.

The methodological assumptions that underpinned this approach included notions that the practitioners could simultaneously work to change practice and take on roles as researchers in communities of learners (Lave and Wenger, 1991); that those working inside the educational contexts of early childhood centres and their managing organisation had significant knowledge about their situation; that they could generate new knowledge, that their workplaces were an appropriate place for inquiry; and that the practitioner is a knower rather than simply a technician, consumer and transmitter of other people's knowledge. We subscribed to Cochran-Smith and Lytle's (2009: 45) contention that practitioners are 'wise consumers of a reservoir of [educational] products' and believed that the CRG members had the capacity to inform and shape their own work. A systematic and intentional study was planned that included cycles of data collection and analysis. Finally, by now making this work public, we hope to both fulfil one of the recognised characteristics of practitioner research (Cochran-Smith and Lytle, 2009) to make local research public to inform, and be critiqued and challenged by others.

The practitioner research presented in this chapter is 'grounded fundamentally in the dialectic of inquiry and practice rather than in one particular theoretical tradition' (Cochran-Smith and Lytle, 2009: 43), but was framed by the introduction of the Early Years Learning Framework (EYLF) (Department of Education Employment and Workplace Relations, 2009) in Australia, which commenced during the CRG implementation. This national curriculum framework is explicit about its eclectic underpinning theoretical influences of developmental, sociocultural, socio-behaviourist, critical and post-structural theories (Department of Education Employment and Workplace Relations, 2009) and the expectation of pedagogical leadership. Our working understanding of pedagogical leadership is that 'pedagogical leadership can only be actualised within the limits of the leader's pedagogic consciousness. This assumption underlines the leader's own action in view of her/his pedagogic goals and/or in relation to the pedagogic principles applied by the staff' (Nivala and Hujala, 2002: 18). Practitioners were working with these theoretical positions to frame their work.

Methodology

The Jean Denton project was framed by a sociocultural methodology involving the formation of a community of learners as co-constructors of knowledge (Lave and Wenger, 1991), positioning practitioner researchers as capable knowers of their work and context, trying to understand and embrace change (Burdon, 2010). The initial Jean Denton project involved participants attending five semi-structured community of practice sessions, organised six–eight weeks apart during which readings about practitioner inquiry and action research were provided and discussed, research questions were written and projects were planned, implemented and evaluated. A wiki (blog) site was established where readings and group discussions were held between meetings. The meetings began with trigger questions designed to provoke discussion relevant to the stage of participants' studies. The researchers shared their project ideas, challenges, confusions and frustrations. During the meetings, as well as online, participants co-constructed new understandings about practitioner research and their areas of investigation (Newman and Mowbray, 2012). As the CRG evolved beyond the life of the Jean Denton project it continued to adopt key elements of this approach and as it evolved, regular meetings continued.

Description of study

In its initial phase as part of the Jean Denton project, the CRG collected data from educators in six early childhood centres through a survey asking how they implemented curriculum, planned for individuals and groups and what kind of documentation was used to record curriculum practices. Participants were also asked to keep a reflective journal, to participate in whole team discussions and one-to-one interviews and to provide samples of curriculum documentation prior to and at the conclusion of the research project. In response to initial findings, the CRG developed training and resources to support contemporary curriculum documentation practices in a deliberate attempt to resonate and engage with educators. The group sought to engender a sense of renewal, to restore, replenish and find vibrancy in educator practice and engagement with curriculum. When establishing the membership of the CRG the participation of educators across the organisation was promoted by having a diversity of representatives including members of the management team and educators from centres. The final group included a children's services coordinator (Kim), two centre directors (including Trish), and an early childhood teacher.

Janet, Kim and Trish recognised that joining the Jean Denton practitioner inquiry project provided an opportunity to gain valuable data
about current staff capacities and to help identify ways forward for training and support. The CRG study aimed to identify current curriculum
practices at services, and educator's capacities in relation to curriculum.
Action research cycles across the six long day care and preschool centres
involved monthly training, initially based on survey findings, delivered
to volunteer centre curriculum facilitators by the CRG. These curriculum facilitators delivered training to the centre teams at team meetings
throughout the initial six months. Ongoing modules were developed iter-
atively, based on feedback at each session. At the end of this period the
survey was repeated and analysed. We next discuss the realisation that
'training' was inconsistent with the philosophy of practitioner research,
and how the CRG was amended accordingly.

At the completion of the Jean Denton project the CRG was extended
to about 250 educators across 23 centres. As the research study gathered
momentum the CRG began to recognise the shortcomings in their initial
training model and develop a more reflexive framework for documentation of curriculum that reflected contemporary early childhood practices as
elaborated in the national Early Years Learning Framework (Department of
Education Employment and Workplace Relations, 2009), which was new
at that time. The CRG framework was defined as reflection and action (or
reflexion), which develops actions to change behaviours, dispositions,
attitudes and knowledge systematically within collegial conversations
(Yelland et al., 2008). It was critical that the framework and documentation were user friendly, would provide consistency, underpin everyday
practice, encourage reflexivity, provide for responsiveness to centre and
community culture and assist educators to articulate theory, their pedagogical leadership and practice with confidence.

The CRG framework was developed by members using existing documents including the current state regulations, City Council and Children's
Services policies, the Children's Services Vision/Mission statement and
the NSW Curriculum Framework (current at the time), with much debate,
reflection, provocation and collaboration. Reflecting back now, Trish and
Janet see the role of the university academic, Linda, in this process of
reflection and framework development as critical, and acknowledge the
warm and reciprocal relationship that developed in which the expertise
of all individuals including the direct practice of the early childhood educators was recognised.

Once developed, the framework was used as the basis for further action.
Having identified the futility of expecting one-off training sessions to

have a significant impact on practice, the design of the delivery of training sessions was carefully considered. The CRG developed training modules that could be implemented by educators at monthly team meetings. Each service nominated an educator (a curriculum facilitator) to attend monthly sessions where the training was delivered and the curriculum facilitator then delivered the training to her staff team at their next team meeting. Careful selection of the curriculum facilitator at each site ensured the facilitator had relevant expertise and experience in early childhood curriculum and the confidence to deliver training. Mentoring educators to gain further skills in these areas was also an embedded part of the CRG process. Survey findings from the initial study indicated that educators lacked understanding about the philosophies that underpinned contemporary planning. Responding to survey findings, the initial sessions focused on communicating the CRG framework to educators and the delivery of sessions aimed at improving their understanding in relation to contemporary early childhood practice and philosophy and their place in planning.

Issues and challenges

Although completion of the surveys for the research project was undertaken at centres during paid team sessions, there was reluctance on the part of a small number of educators to participate and it seemed likely they would choose not to if the exercise was not part of their employment. This reluctance to fully engage with the process of curriculum renewal continued for a small number of educators in some services and was consistently reported by Curriculum Facilitators as their biggest challenge in the delivery of training sessions and mentoring of educators. Embedding training as a recurring part of team meetings ensured that all educators continued to be part of the curriculum renewal process and to be influenced by the perspectives presented regardless of their personal engagement with the material. The CRG is now in its sixth year and engaging all educators in the process is still consistently reported as the biggest challenge by the facilitators.

In response to this issue, a move towards a more participatory and collaborative model was instituted in 2012. Janet and Trish realised at this time that the model was a largely 'top-down' training and needed to become more participatory. The CRG process was amended to incorporate a more interactive style of professional learning in which services were guided through their own action research projects, including choosing a curriculum area to work with, developing an action plan to extend this area and presentation of their centre journey at a staffing showcase for all services.

This approach was more successful at engaging greater numbers of staff and the use of a detailed action plan ensured that all staff at a site contributed to curriculum renewal, resulting in everyone being better engaged with the process. The confidence and expertise to support educators to develop and manage their own research project lay in the lessons learnt by the CRG in the development and implementation of their project with support from Linda. Our experience with the success of this amended approach reflects Early's (2010) contention that 'one-shot' professional development is unlikely to be very effective and that, alternatively, effectiveness is linked to ongoing immersion in a collaborative community of inquiry.

This style of planning had positive outcomes at a centre level. The CRG training supported the facilitator to work with her centre educators to develop a centre research project in an area of their own interest. For example, a number of services selected sustainable practice and spent the year working through an action plan they created as a group to extend their understandings and practices in this area. Subsequently some of these services became leaders in this area of curriculum and provided training, centre visits and information to other centres. This in turn built their own centre's knowledge and leadership.

One of the major challenges, frequently discussed, was time – time for the CRG to come together, time to train the curriculum facilitators and time for the facilitators to pass on their knowledge and engage the educators at their service. It had been determined that the best way to do the latter was at the centre monthly team meetings. However, with an overcrowded agenda, time for curriculum was tight and some facilitators felt an inability to meaningfully engage with their team on curriculum, diminishing the impact and ability to create a sense of renewal and revitalisation. This challenge was mainly overcome by stripping the staff meeting agenda of items that could be addressed via other means and prioritising curriculum as the number one topic.

One of the major benefits of a collaboration between management and practitioners was evident as management responded to the issue of time for centre-based educators to plan, evaluate and reflect, especially completing required documentation. They made new provision for regular time release so educators could be released from the rooms for 'programming' and curriculum related tasks and projects. Combined with the regularly embedded training, this has had a significant, positive impact on educators, upon whom day-to-day curriculum implementation depends. Educators have demonstrated a greater knowledge and understanding in assessing and documenting children's learning.

However, it was clear that it would take more than staff meetings to fully engage all educators in processes of curriculum renewal. One of the challenges was that educators often felt a sense of isolation from other early childhood professionals and lacked support from the management team. One educator who was surveyed for the study said, 'I feel isolated from my peers and feel like I'm doing this on my own'.

A series of networking and showcase opportunities was devised to run alongside the curriculum renewal training. We found that this inspired and motivated educators and promoted the development of positive professional relationships. The role of curriculum facilitator and membership of the CRG are now desirable positions and there is keen interest from educators to fill these positions when they become vacant.

Although staff turnover in the organisation falls below the national average for the sector in Australia, the progression of curriculum renewal was impacted when curriculum facilitators left. Training others to take on the role effectively was a challenge for the renewal team. This was mainly addressed by assigning mentors and a buddy system with experienced and new facilitators who visited each other's centres and staff meetings for mutual support, feedback and encouragement.

Findings

The data collected from initial surveys, reflective journals and interviews confirmed the observations that had informed the formation of the CRG. The majority of respondents indicated that they implemented an emergent curriculum at their centres but 41 per cent could not identify the documents they used to record planning. The data also showed that educators planned primarily for individuals with a focus on developmentally appropriate practice. In addition the survey administered at the beginning of the CRG process revealed that the influence of the centre director, and whether this person was recently degree qualified or an early childhood teacher who had continued on the journey of personal professional development, was a determining factor in how contemporary the curriculum implementation was. This confirmed for the CRG that our focus on collaboratively developing an accessible reflexive planning framework was critical and also supported the design of the collaborative research communities that demonstrated the effect curriculum facilitators could have on service provision. This supports previous research about the benefits of ongoing collaborative learning models (Campbell, 2003; Early, 2010).

At the completion of the six month Jean Denton study, the surveys showed that the training sessions were having an effect and educators were feeling more confident about curriculum delivery and demonstrated a better understanding of contemporary practice. This gave the CRG confidence that the format of the training delivered was showing positive results and the CRG and the regular roll out of training to services continued and grew to include the additional 17 centres. The value of the study was not only in confirming understanding of the practice of educators in centres but in developing a model for the creation and delivery of training that regularly sought feedback from the Curriculum Facilitators and the educators in centres to assess its value and effectiveness and ensuring any feedback received was used in the further development of training sessions.

The continuation of the CRG using this format has had significant consequences for the provision of programmes in the organisations' centres and these years also marked a time of change across the early childhood sector. In 2008 the training focus was on contemporary early childhood philosophies including the role of sociocultural theory in curriculum development. This training placed educators and services in an excellent position to begin to understand and implement the principles and practices of the Early Years Learning Framework (EYLF), *Belonging, Being & Becoming* (Department of Education Employment and Workplace Relations, 2009) when it was introduced in 2009. From this point forward the CRG used the EYLF as the framework for the development of the monthly training sessions delivered to staff teams. This meant that an understanding of the document and how to embed it into centre practice was well established by our services by the time our new accreditation system, the National Quality Standard (NQS) (Australian Children's Education and Care Quality Authority, 2013) was released to the sector. With the receipt of the NQS, the CRG used the EYLF and the NQS to frame the development of training sessions, always using feedback from services and educators to inform its creation. Once assessment and rating visits began under the NQS the staff development process that began with the Jean Denton study and continued through the CRG began to show quantifiable results, with the number of our services that received a rating of meeting or exceeding the standard being well above the national average.

The CRG continues and gains strength through ongoing monitoring of curriculum implementation that occurs both formally and informally to measure changes in the beliefs, attitudes and practices of educators. Each year the members collaborate to redesign the content of the curriculum renewal implementation which is adapted in response to participant feedback and evaluated by the CRG annually. Supporting centres to develop site-based (situated) research projects each year has allowed each centre to extend its skill, understanding and practices in curriculum areas it feels are important to its children, families and local communities. Direct feedback from educators about the training and process of curriculum renewal has included the following statements:

I feel more confident.

I have changed the way I think about curriculum and documentation.

I can confidently discuss what I'm doing and why I'm doing it.

I clearly know what the expectations are in relation to documentation.

Conclusions and insights gained

Trish

At the beginning of the project I was the director/teacher of a long day care service attended by 40 children per day aged six weeks to six years. My participation in this project was the first opportunity I had to work outside of my direct role with children and families. In effect, the first time I had the opportunity to lift my head up from the day-to-day work ahead of me and to think deeply about why I did what I did and what I could do to make it better. At this time I was enrolled at university and was working towards my fourth year as an early childhood teacher. Despite this exposure to an academic environment, during the early meetings to plan the study I often felt overwhelmed and intimidated. At the meetings, Linda supported us to consider the methodology we would use for our study, giving us readings to inform us, but even after reading and discussing them I didn't feel confident about how to move forward. It was the ongoing support from Linda in the early days of the study and the CRG that gave me the confidence to move through the steps of design and implementation of the study and the creation and delivery of the curriculum training modules.

The meetings at the university were initially also intimidating for me as my manager attended them. I did not know Janet well at the time and felt that I needed to demonstrate intelligence and knowledge to justify my inclusion in the group and I had little of either in relation to research. However, working together allowed me to understand that Janet was not 'sitting in judgement' on me but working with me to understand and design and implement our study. Over the six years that I have now been a member of the CRG my relationship with Janet has changed as we worked together through numerous projects and challenges. It is now a very respectful professional relationship where we both know and acknowledge the other's strengths and skills.

Looking back to the beginning of the study is difficult because so much has changed and professionally I feel a completely different person. My membership of the CRG has continued and my role in the group has grown. When I first started in the group I was a contributing member and completed what was asked of me. Now I take an active leadership role in the group and it is my hope that I have contributed to the continued success and influence of it. During my membership I have gained skill and confidence in designing and delivering training to educators and I have a particular interest in using teaching strategies that engage and empower staff. I am driven to design professional learning that allows educators to take control of their learning and this drive is embedded in the knowledge gained through the initial study and the continual process of design, delivery and evaluation that have been underlying principles of the CRG thanks to our collaboration through the first years with Linda.

In 2011 I was seconded to a position with Children's Services for six months that was aimed at providing pedagogical leadership to educators and their services in curriculum development. As part of the project I visited services, developed support materials for the documentation of learning and delivered targeted training. This six-month position was a personal revelation to me. I had been very dedicated to working directly with children and their families but through this project I realised the powerful role I could play in their lives by working with educators and supporting them to reflect upon their practice.

In 2012 the National Quality Standard (Australian Children's Education and Care Quality Authority, 2013) was introduced across Australia and early childhood centres were to receive assessment and rating visits that would measure their performance against the standard. It was a time of great change to the early childhood profession in NSW and I was again seconded by Children's Services to support our centres to understand and implement the standard to prepare for their assessment and rating visits. I have worked in this position now for two years and my understanding, skill and confidence have grown enormously. I have continued my studies throughout this time and am currently writing the thesis for my Master of Education (Early Childhood).

Janet

An essential mutual understanding underpinning this project was that the educator, academic and manager were all recognised as possessing expert knowledge in differing forms. Educators have experiential knowledge, know their centres, their peers, their children and their community. The academic is an experienced researcher, with

(Continued)

(Continued)

research knowledge and knows what is deemed to be important in supporting curriculum implementation (Gore and Gitlin, 2004). As the manager I was aware of the bigger picture including the Children's Services Department and organisational expectations. At the heart of the project was the synergy that came from the combination of these areas of expert knowledge. Collaboration between research participants resulted in everyone being willing to share and learn from each other, ongoing negotiation and, over time, the development of trust. The growth and development of confidence of practitioners in unchartered waters such as research was a joy to behold.

As the implementation of curriculum renewal entered its second and subsequent years, a greater number of participants at all levels wanted to be more active and assume greater personal responsibility for the quality of curriculum implementation at their centre. As time went on, participants were empowered by the realisation that they could make significant change and share their own understandings with their peers and with parents of children attending their service. The project overall generated greater collaboration within and between services and among educators.

From a management perspective, having the commitment and enthusiasm for curriculum renewal in a key member of the management team (Kim Nasner) and a degree qualified centre supervisor/teacher (Trish) has ensured sustainability over time. Even with staff turnover at the centre level and Kim's departure from the team, our curriculum renewal continued and grows from strength to strength. Supported by the framework of the CRG we have been able to deliver a diverse range of projects that have enriched our curriculum delivery including training, mentoring and support to understand and work with attachment theory and the Art Kids Project, which involved an aboriginal artist working with children to develop their knowledge of creative arts. What this study has demonstrated is that with initial key enablers and drivers (the manager, centre supervisor and the academic) and engagement with others over time with similar passion, tenacity and drive, projects such as this one can be sustained.

Linda

As an academic and former preschool teacher, looking back over the more than six years that I have been learning about and working in practitioner research, I see many challenges and, overwhelmingly, rewards. In 2008 when I ventured into my first university facilitated practitioner research, I myself was a new learner in this area and felt excited about the prospects of practitioners designing and leading their own research and change. The pragmatic challenges such as time, staff illnesses and centre and school management issues were fairly overwhelming among the group and attrition was high. Among the five projects that continued, however, including the CRG, the achievements and opportunities for sustainability were exciting (Newman and Mowbray, 2012).

When I accepted the invitation from Janet, Kim and Trish to move from Jean Denton project leader to collaborative CRG member I was nervous about the real contributions I could make, as my teaching experience in a centre was many years in the past. I had become much more used to being a lecturer and manager. Initially I struggled to 'bite my tongue' in the shift in power relationship from tutor, rightly or wrongly considered by some to be hierarchically higher than the practitioner role (Gore and Gitlin, 2004), to equal participant in a learning community. There was a temptation to say 'this is how you should do it' when we were discussing something I regularly lectured on, or knew about from academic research or literature. The rewards came though as others offered great ideas that I hadn't thought about, and the planning process moved forward. I was able to learn more about the current realities of daily life in services, and the management of a large service provider. These are all valuable lessons for my university teaching and research. It is deeply gratifying to see that the work commenced with Janet, Kim and Trish is continuing in the long term and has resulted in so many tangible gains in individual services and the organisation as a whole.

Reflecting on the current time, I can now see how this early experience was influential in my own career trajectory too. I have since moved into a promotion position at a new university, and engaged in a practitioner research project in my new region (Newman, under review), and in Chile (see Chapter 2). I am now a passionate advocate for PR as a sustainable form of professional learning that is qualitatively superior to 'one-hit' staff development programmes.

Together we agree on the substantial and sustainable changes that have grown from our relationship and work together. As a practitioner research community of learners we were stronger together than apart. We each brought different knowledge, skills and understandings to the group and project. Our challenges must not be forgotten, however. In each of our jobs we were challenged to find enough time for the work, and it was our belief in the benefits of the project and

(Continued)

(Continued)

trust in each other that kept us going. Real costs were hidden, with Linda working in an unfunded capacity and Janet and Trish each squeezing hours from their long list of responsibilities. There were initially challenges in lack of 'buy in' by some practitioners in centres, which were later overcome by making the research more participatory and practitioner lead, fully supporting the literature on practitioner research that advocates for the benefits of projects that recognised practitioners as 'knowers' (Gore and Gitlin, 2004). Each of us has experienced career rewards through promotion, leadership opportunities, new project opportunities and the rewards that come with increasing quality in the organisation. Our ultimate reward is to see the ongoing sustainability of the curriculum renewal and action to increase quality delivery for children and families.

Ongoing research considerations

- As a reader of this chapter, are you searching for a change in your professional identity? Could practitioner research be the key?
- What area of curriculum would you like to begin changing in your workplace through use of practitioner research?

References

Arthur, L., Beecher, B., Death, E., Dockett, S. and Farmer, S. (2008) *Programming and Planning in Early Childhood Settings* (4th edn). Melbourne: Thomson.

Australian Children's Education and Care Quality Authority (2013) *Guide to the National Quality Standard*. Retrieved from: http://files.acecqa.gov.au/files/National-Quality-Framework-Resources-Kit/NQF03-Guide-to-NQS-130902.pdf (last accessed 25 November 2014).

Burdon, K. (2010) 'Conceptualising teachers' professional learning with Web 2.0', *Campus-Wide Information Systems*, 27 (3): 148–61.

Campbell, A. (2003) 'Teachers' concerns and professional development in England: some questions, issues and concerns', *Journal of In-Service Education*, 29 (3): 375–88.

Cochran-Smith, M. and Lytle. S. (2009) 'Teacher research as stance', in S. Noffke and B. Somekh (eds), *The Sage Handbook of Educational Action Research*. London: Sage, pp. 39–49.

Department of Education Employment and Workplace Relations (2009) *Belonging, Being & Becoming: The Early Years Learning Framework for Australia*. Barton, ACT: Council of Australian Governments/Commonwealth of Australia.

Early, P. (2010) 'Continuing professional development of teachers', *International Encyclopedia of Education* (3rd edn), pp. 207–13. Retrieved from: www. sciencedirect.com.ezproxy.newcastle.edu.au/science/article/pii/B97800 80448947010770# (last accessed 29 October 2014).

Edwards, S. (2007) 'Theoretical transitions and professional learning: how do early childhood teachers understand sociocultural theory?', *New Zealand Research in Early Childhood Education Journal*, 10: 131–44.

Gore, J. and Gitlin, A. (2004) '[Re]Visioning the academic-teacher divide: power and knowledge in the educational community', *Teachers and Teaching: Theory and Practice*, 10 (1): 35–58.

Jones, E. and Nimmo, J. (1994) *Emergent Curriculum*. Washington, DC: National Association for the Education of Young Children.

Lave, J. and Wenger, E. (1991) *Legitimate Peripheral Participation: Situated Learning*. Cambridge: Cambridge University Press.

Newman, L. (under review) *Children's Literacy Play Environments: Snapshots of Teacher Change*.

Newman, L. and Mowbray, S. (2012) '"We were expected to be equal": teachers and academics sharing professional learning through practitioner inquiry', *Teachers and Teaching: Theory and Practice*, 18 (4): 455–68.

Nivala, V. and Hujala, E. (eds) (2002) *Leadership in Early Childhood Education: Cross Cultural Perspectives*. Oulu: University of Oulu.

NSW Department of Community Services, Office of Childcare (2001) *NSW Curriculum Framework for Children's Services: The Practice of Relationships*. Sydney: NSW Department of Community Services.

Yelland, N., Lee, L., O'Rourke, M. and Harrison, C. (2008) *Rethinking Learning in Early Childhood*. Berkshire: McGraw Hill Open University Press.

8

(IN)SIGHTS FROM 40 YEARS OF PRACTITIONER ACTION RESEARCH IN EDUCATION: PERSPECTIVES FROM THE US, UK AND AUSTRALIA

Nicole Mockler and Ashley Casey

Key words   reflexive inquiry; evidence-based practice; practitioner research; praxis.

Chapter overview

This book advocates practitioner research as a vehicle for transformation and change in early childhood settings. This chapter draws on the rich history of practitioner research in schools to suggest some (in)sights – both personal (in) and theoretical (sights) – gained over the past 40 years of practitioner action research in education that might be salient for early childhood educators embarking on practitioner research. In the first part, we provide a brief history of practitioner inquiry and action research in schools, drawing on traditions developed in the United States, United Kingdom and Australia. In the second section, we contrast these traditions with the recent 'evidence-based practice' turn in education, arguing that the best practitioner action research is critical, emancipatory, contextual and generative, focusing on problematisation of practice as opposed to solving either real or 'manufactured' problems. We then draw on our personal experiences – as practitioner researchers and academic partners to practitioner researchers in school contexts – to provide illustrations of approaches to practitioner action research that, we consider, move beyond 'evidence-based practice', before concluding with some observations that we hope might support our early childhood colleagues.

Before we begin, however, a note about terminology. A useful summary of the way the term 'practitioner research' is used was given by Cochran-Smith and Lytle (2007: 25), who described it as 'a conceptual and linguistic umbrella to refer to a wide array of education research modes, forms, genres, and purposes'. They argued that the expression encompasses a range of educational research methods such as: action research; teacher research; self-study; narrative (or autobiographical) inquiry; the scholarship of teaching and learning; and the use of teaching as a context for research (Cochran-Smith and Lytle, 2007). In a comparable article Zeichner and Noffke (2001: 7) made their own list of practitioner research traditions that developed through decades of 'evolution and contestation'. These include: 'the action research tradition; the British teacher-as-researcher movement and the participatory action research movement in Australia; and the teacher researcher movement in North America'.

It is the US, UK and Australian traditions that we pay particular attention to in this chapter. That is not to say that expressions of action research developed elsewhere are not noteworthy or significant but that, in providing a background to practitioner research, these contexts afford us enough scope to explore the traditions that have most influenced our own experiences of and beliefs about practitioner research.

Practitioner research in schools: historical perspectives

The historical roots of practitioner research are complex and multifaceted, and have been illustrated in detail in a number of other writings (see, for example, Groundwater-Smith and Mockler, 2009; Noffke, 1997). Rather than a comprehensive history, our intention in this short section is to take an historical perspective in contrasting traditions in practitioner research from different geographical contexts, by way of providing a background to contemporary expressions of practitioner research.

The earliest roots of practitioner research in the US can be seen in the work of Dewey and Corey (from the early twentieth century and 1950s, respectively) in relation to education, and more broadly to the work of

Collier and Lewin in the 1930s and 1940s. Lewin was particularly influential in shaping contemporary understanding in his definition of action research as 'comparative research on the conditions and effects of various forms of social action, and research leading to social action' (Lewin, 1946: 202–3). The 'mainstreaming' of action research in the US, both educational and otherwise, was fuelled by the critical social movements of the second half of the twentieth century including the civil rights and feminist movements, and aimed to provide a challenge to dominant paradigms of both educational research and teacher education (Noffke, 1994, 1997). In other words, it sought to challenge the assumption that '[the primary purpose of educational research] is to establish new generalizations stated as observed uniformities, explanatory principles, or scientific laws' (Corey, 1949: 509), and reposition research as something that challenges, and consequently improves, practice.

The US 'teacher research movement' (Noffke, 1994), which flourished in the late 1980s, has been categorised by Cochran-Smith and Lytle (1999: 17–19) under five broad trends, namely:

- the prominence of teacher research in teacher education, professional development and school reform
- the development of conceptual frameworks for teacher research
- theorising teacher research as social inquiry
- theorising teacher research as ways of knowing in communities, and
- theorising teacher research as practical inquiry.

Cochran-Smith and Lytle (1999) argue that these iterations of action research in the US are connected into the work of scholars such as Ann Berthoff (1987) and other authors whose work was represented in the influential collection, *Reclaiming the Classroom: Teacher Research as an Agency for Change* (Goswami and Stillman, 1987), while at the same time drawing on work developed during the same period and earlier by scholars working in the UK and Australian contexts, as discussed below. While the US tradition in teacher research shares much with the Stenhousian approach developed in the UK (Stenhouse, 1983) and the critical emancipatory approach developed in Australia around the same time (Carr and Kemmis, 1986), both discussed at some length below, where the US approach differs is in the emphasis on individual teachers engaging in research endeavours as opposed to the strongly participatory and collaborative approaches developed elsewhere.

Although action research waned in the US in the 1960s, its fortunes rose once again in the UK shortly afterwards (Zeichner, 2001). Elliott (1997) posits that action research in education emerged in the UK as a way of overcoming the disillusionment of a swathe of young people as a result of the Education Act of 1944. This Act created two types of schools in the UK and allocated the majority of eleven-year-olds to one or other of them. The grammar school catered for the academically elite, some of whom would progress along an academic route towards educational excellence and the university. The mainstream schools, the second-ary modern, were for those deemed 'unsuited' for academic learning. Consequently there emerged a large disaffected student population who were set on leaving school at the age of 15 to complete their passage to the workplace and thus adulthood (Elliott, 1997, 2007).

This disaffected body often saw the subjects that they were taught, par-ticularly the humanities, as irrelevant to the adult world that they would enter. Elliott (2007) concluded that teachers of humanities (i.e. history and geography) had two choices: either develop a system that controlled and contained their students, or restructure the curriculum so that it was seen as relevant. It was those who decided on the path of curriculum restructuring that Elliott (1997) credits with the emergence of action research.

Many (for example, Elliott, 2007; Zeichner, 2001) attribute the 'intro-duction of a radically different theory of knowledge to teachers of the humanities' (Elliott, 2007: 18) to Lawrence Stenhouse. Zeichner (2001) identifies a number of key curriculum reform projects – most notably Stenhouse's 'Humanities Curriculum Project' and the 'Ford Teaching Project' and the work of Elliott – as key factors in the development of action research in UK education. It was through action research that these projects were able to move towards a pedagogically-driven rather than standards or objectives-based curriculum, in which the process became dependent upon teachers' ability to reflect on their practice (Zeichner, 2001).

The key contribution of Stenhouse was to articulate a theory of praxis that supported teachers in translating educational aims into teaching reality (Elliott, 1991, 2007). From this Stenhouse developed his idea of teacher-as-researcher as a means of articulating his wish that teachers develop their pedagogy based upon personal and critical reflection. His work, and that of Elliott, highlighted the impact that action research could have on teachers, and consequently students, especially when teachers were provided with opportunities to critically reflect on their work. However, it also highlighted the need for teachers to reflect and critique not only their personal practice but also the established institutional structures that 'controlled' their working lives.

Australian approaches built very strongly on the work of Stenhouse and others, with an additional emphasis placed on the critical, eman-cipatory and indeed political possibilities of such work (Kemmis and Grundy, 1997). Carr and Kemmis' (1986) ground-breaking work

Becoming Critical: Education, Knowledge and Action Research emphasised the critical dimension of this approach, suggesting that its *raison
d'être* was to challenge the status quo and specifically the dimensions of
the system complicit in the maintenance of systemic inequities. Over the
years, these ideas have been expanded in a variety of directions including teacher professional learning and development (Groundwater-Smith,
1998; Grundy, 1995), and the significance of collaborative inquiry as a
dimension of authentic critical action research (Grundy, 1994; Sachs,
1999). In recent years, Kemmis (2011) has posited a new definition of
critical, participatory action research, which in many ways encapsulates
the Australian tradition. Paraphrased, Kemmis' definition involves the
following:

- collective research undertaken by participants in a social practice to
  achieve 'effective historical consciousness' of their practice as *praxis*
- a process in which participants engage in critical and self-critical
  reflection on their praxis, individually and collectively; their historically formed and intersubjective understandings of practice; and
  the historically formed fields that constitute the conditions of their
  practice
- a process whereby 'communicative space' is opened – wherein shared
  insights and decisions might be developed in relation to the evolution
  of practice and the tensions and interconnections between *system* and
  lifeworld (Habermas, 1987)
- an enterprise in which participants investigate reality in order to transform it, and conversely, transform reality in order to investigate it
- an enterprise with both practical aims and emancipatory aims.

This approach, then, is about engagement with and evolution of *praxis*,
defined as morally informed action, as a collaborative enterprise with
both practical and liberatory aims.

The Australian tradition stands on the shoulders of both early iterations
in the US and the work in the UK. We do not suggest, however, that practitioner research undertaken in Australian schools (or indeed elsewhere)
meets the aspirational aims as laid out by Kemmis. One of the potential
challenges to the realisation of these aims is the current emphasis on
'evidence-based practice'. In the next section we explore some of the contemporary pressures on practitioner research and practitioner researchers
resulting from the neoliberal education policy context within which they
practise, followed by some reflections on our own experiences of practitioner research in schools from both the UK and Australia, which might
be seen to swim against the tide.

The 'evidence-based practice' turn in practitioner research

The current iteration of evidence-based practice in education can be traced to Hargreaves' Teacher Training Agency lecture of 1996 (subsequently Hargreaves, 2007). Hargreaves lamented the lack of 'value for money' in publicly funded educational research, calling for teachers to engage in applied educational research similar to that engaged in by the medical profession, focusing their research efforts on 'what works' in the classroom, so as to determine and subsequently disperse 'best practice'. In a comparison between educational and medical professions in terms of their use of 'evidence', he found teaching to be largely deficient:

> Today teachers still have to discover or adopt most of their own professional practices by personal preference, guided by neither the accumulated wisdom of seniors nor by practitioner-relevant research. They see no need to keep abreast of research developments and rightly regard research journals as being directed to fellow academics, not to them. (Hargreaves, 2007: 7)

As former teachers we would argue that Hargreaves' comments hit close to the mark. However, what we do refute is his simplistic assertion that what teachers do badly the medical profession does well. The key problem, however, with Hargreaves' argument is the exceptional lack of clarity around what constitutes appropriate evidence in education, and the key differences between this and the kind of evidence that serves medical practitioners well in their work. Hargreaves' call for teaching to become an 'evidence-based' profession rivalling medicine belies a simplistic understanding of the relationship between 'evidence' and scientific certainty.

Hargreaves' advocacy of 'what works' was subsequently critiqued by a range of scholars, such as Elliott (2001) and Hammersley (1997), who argued against the narrow definition of 'evidence' upon which his argument was predicated, maintaining that 'a narrow focus on "what works" will close the door that leads to new possibilities, new strategies, new ways of reframing and reconceiving the educational enterprise' (Atkinson, 2000: 328). Writing in a similar vein, albeit before Hargreaves, Carr (1980: 66) suggested that educational theory should:

> emancipate practitioners from their dependence on practices that are the product of precedent, habit and tradition by developing modes of analysis and enquiry that are aimed at exposing and examining beliefs, values and assumptions implicit in the theoretical framework through which practitioners organise their experience.

While initially this iteration of evidence-based practice emerged from the UK, there has been an increased focus on evidence-based practice in the US (Slavin, 2002), in the years since the re-authorisation of the Elementary and Secondary Education Act in 2001 (known as 'No Child Left Behind') in the United States. A focus on 'scientifically-based educational research' (Eisenhart and Towne, 2003), privileging randomised controlled trials as the 'gold standard' (Biesta, 2014) in educational research, has emerged as increasingly preferred, to the exclusion of other approaches to research, re-shaping over time the landscape of educational research in the US (Lather, 2010).

In Australia, the notion of evidence-based practice has been embedded in federal policy documents such as *Belonging, Being & Becoming: The Early Years Learning Framework* (Department of Education Employment and Workplace Relations, 2009) and the *Australian Teacher Performance and Development Framework* (Australian Institute for Teaching and School Leadership, 2012b). Additionally, it also underpins processes such as teacher registration and certification, where teachers are required 'to evidence' (Australian Institute for Teaching and School Leadership, 2012a) their practice in annotatable, demonstrable responses to the Australian Professional Standards for Teachers, reminiscent of the approach to teaching standards taken in the UK.

In the UK evidence-based practice has made a growing re-entry into public discourse around education since 2010. In particular, a series of commissioned reviews and reports have sought to provide a rationale for the uptake of evidence-based practice. The most significant of these, 'Building Evidence into Education', was commissioned in 2013 by Michael Gove, then Education Secretary, and conducted by epidemiologist Ben Goldacre. Goldacre (2013) argued for the adoption of randomised controlled trials by teachers (and presumably, other educational researchers), while using the concept of 'evidence-based practice' interchangeably with that of randomised controlled trials. Clearly for Goldacre, the evidence that 'counts' is that generated through randomised controlled trials, and, similar to Hargreaves, the question of what actually constitutes *good* evidence remains unaddressed. Additionally, the different contexts of scientific and social research and 'evidence' and the implications of these differences also remain ignored. As one of us has recently claimed:

> the suggestion that 'what works', when arrived at through this narrow interpretation and use of evidence, will provide a catalyst for the teaching profession to become more enlightened and evolved betrays a deep misunderstanding of the current scope and shape of teachers' work, the role of professional judgement and joint enterprise in that work, and the context within which teachers' work is enacted. (Mockler and Groundwater-Smith, 2015a: 43)

Fundamentally, we question how far randomised controlled trials can be regarded as the 'gold standard' or 'one true path' when applied to situations, such as schools, where the key players (i.e. teachers and the students) are neither randomised nor controlled.

We are reminded here of the words of Kemmis (2006: 459):

> Much of the action research that has proliferated in many parts of the world over the past two decades has not been the vehicle for educational critique we hoped it would be. Instead, some may even have become a vehicle for domesticating students and teachers to conventional forms of schooling.

Our own experiences of practitioner research in the field, however, stand largely contrary to this, and it is to some of the ways in which we have experienced this work that we now turn.

Practitioner research in schools: our stories

Ashley worked for 15 years as a physical education (PE) teacher in the UK and undertook a longitudinal approach to pedagogical and curriculum change through practitioner research. Over a seven-year period, across multiple classes, topics and ability groupings, he engaged in an insider study (i.e. as a teacher-as-researcher). Nicole began her career as a secondary history and English teacher, and over the past 20 years has engaged in practitioner research as a teacher and a teacher educator, while also working in a variety of different school contexts to support teachers in their engagement with practitioner inquiry and other forms of professional learning.

Insider out – Ashley

Drawing on wider research in PE I wonder if the subject has operated for decades under a type of 'evidence-based' approach to teaching. Nothing to me epitomises this process more than 'teaching' in track and field athletics. The common experiences I hear from my teacher education students is that athletics was about two things: a) measuring times, distances or heights, and then b) picking teams for sports day. Children are asked, year-on-year, to perform to their maximum ability, with improvement on testing equated to learning (which, of course, children often do as they mature – improve that is). Subsequently they are then taught how to better pass the test (i.e. improve their measurements), and the cycle begins again. Indeed, before I used action research the only outcome of my teaching was improved performance; after all, this was what 'everyone else' was doing. Indeed, Tinning (1991) argued that this technocratic rationality is the dominant *trade wind* pedagogy in PE against which every other idea must blow.

Importantly, practice in PE has repeatedly been described as traditional. Many have argued that, at its core, practice has changed little in the last 50 years (Kirk, 2011; Tinning, 2012). The place of the teacher-as-teller is firmly established, as is the importance placed on technical competence and competition. Those who are good at these aspects of physical education *ergo* 'team sports' – and that is the lens through which competence is often judged – thrive, while those who are not have to try to survive. PE is one of those polarising 'Dr Pepper' subjects (you either love it or you hate it) and PE (HPE in Australia) has long lived with this moniker.

Unsurprisingly, I loved PE (I still do but for different reasons). I thrived in team games and showed technical competence in everything – except dance, and as that wasn't a medium through which competence was judged I was quite safe. I didn't get close in other subjects and school was a place where I went to 'do' sport and survive class – the complete reverse of many I am sure. Unsurprisingly this is the notion of PE I brought with me when I started teaching and, unsurprisingly, my own students subsequently either thrived or looked to survive.

It was against this background, working in a school that had hundreds of years of history of valuing this type of physical activity, that I discovered action research through a part-time Masters degree. Interestingly I was not enamoured with it at first. It was starkly different from the 'sport science' I had studied at university, and challenged my expectations about doing research. Yet as I grew into it I started to understand its potential. The ability to make changes to my practice and enhance my students' learning was no longer based on a hunch or gut instinct. My 'spider senses' no longer needed to tingle (well, shake violently – because after decades of privileging technical competence my senses weren't sensitive to anything but a well-executed shot) before I would make a change.

However, and in an effort to change my traditional practice and alter the landscape (for my students) of my 'evidence-based' approach some of my forays into publishing/writing about action research (see Casey, 2013; Casey et al., 2009) explored the use of alternative pedagogical approaches to learning in PE generally (athletics specifically). What I concluded in the most recent was:

In considering pedagogical change, I advocate action research as a means of supporting sustained change (Noffke and Zeichner, 1987;

Zeichner, 2003) and enhancing the normal practices (Feldman, 1996) that occur in the name of physical education. However, while the action research process did act on many occasions to mitigate the suppressed philosophies and habits of my teaching, it is important to note that this was not always possible. Some habits are simply harder to change than others. (Casey, 2013: 160)

Practitioner research helped me to develop my practice but it was not a panacea for all the traditional 'difficulties' in teaching PE. Instead, I had to acknowledge that while there were better ways of teaching – ones that privileged the students' learning over my teaching and expertise (and to which I could aspire) – there was a journey to be taken towards improvement. However, change is not a simple or straightforward process and nor is it something that occurs overnight. Fundamentally, practice in PE (or any subject for that matter) has not developed on a whim and nor will it be changed on one. It is resistant and, as such, I needed to set about reassuring myself that the 'new' was better than the 'old'.

I started small: one unit of work at a time using alternative pedagogical approaches. Often this involved working with multiple classes through the same material (as is often the case with a secondary teacher's timetable) and it was almost exclusively undertaken on my own. In my case these 'new' ways of 'doing' PE were not embraced by my colleagues. It took time to convince them that this was 'proper' teaching and that the students were learning as a consequence of my actions and yet that is what practitioner research allowed me to do. The truth, as I see it, was that the students were learning more, and not just how to pass the test. They were learning beyond the physical and had developed their cognitive, social and affective understanding. These four aspects have been positioned as the legitimate learning outcomes of PE and yet they have also proven elusive outcomes of traditional practice (Casey and Goodyear, 2015). Over time one unit became seven years and three classes became many as I expand my use of these alternative pedagogical approaches. Change didn't occur overnight but over years, but it was fundamentally supported by practitioner research.

Outsider in – Nicole

I came to practitioner research in my sixth year of teaching, drafted onto a school-based team for an externally funded project that was part of the 'Innovation and Best Practice Project' (IBPP) (Cuttance, 2001). The IBPP was one of a number of large-scale funded projects that characterised the practitioner research scene in Australia in the 1990s and early 2000s

(Mockler, 2013), and while working within the constraints of the require-ments of the funding provider was not always easy, the requirement that each school-based team be appointed an academic partner for the pro-ject came as quite an unexpected bonus. Our academic partner came with a deep understanding of the tenets of critical participatory action research, and a strong commitment to teachers' engagement in research as a strategy for the critical, collaborative interrogation of professional practice.

As I engaged with that first practitioner inquiry project, I found myself, perhaps for the first time, entering into both an intellectual and practi-cal examination of my own practice. I remember very well the critical questions about our practice posed by the team and the processes by which we went about positing answers, melding targeted professional reading with the collection of data from our students, our colleagues and other members of the school community. Without wishing to evangelise, the process constituted something of an awakening. As a professional development strategy, it was situated within the context of my current professional concerns and questions; it constituted a deeply collaborative and collegial exercise; and it provided a near perfect combination of the intellectual work involved in reading and assimilating the work of other 'real' researchers along with the practical intellectual work of collecting and analysing our own data.

Sometime later, having engaged in a number of other collaborative practitioner research projects, I found myself appointed to a new school, wherein my particular responsibility was the fostering and supporting of teacher professional learning and development. The establishment of a culture of inquiry within the school was a central piece of this work, and over the next six years I worked alongside teachers in a broad range of configurations to support them in investigating their practice and seeking both 'welcome' and 'unwelcome truths' (Mockler and Groundwater-Smith, 2015b). In the subsequent decade, I have worked as academic partner to teachers in over 20 schools on both funded and unfunded projects, sup-porting them to engage in inquiry for the purposes of professional develop-ment and advancement of collective practice, and also as academic partner to the Coalition of Knowledge Building Schools, a network of schools in Sydney committed to inquiry-based professional learning and practice.

Over the years this has involved work as diverse as:

- providing hands-on workshops on methods of data collection and analysis for teachers
- supporting practitioner researchers to generate research questions and shape and focus their inquiries

- constructing reading lists and drawing together resources for practitioner researchers to access
- undertaking preliminary data analysis to allow practitioner researchers to focus on 'making sense of the data' in their (often limited) collaborative time
- on occasion, undertaking data collection on practitioner researchers' behalf (for example, where teachers feel that it would be best for focus groups to be run by an 'outsider')
- bringing an 'outside' perspective to the task of 'making sense' of data gathered by practitioner researchers.

My experience across a range of school contexts suggests that practitioner action research can work as a powerful catalyst for professional learning, bringing practitioners into collaborative dialogue about their practice and the problems and issues it proffers. In these neoliberal times where the call to be 'data driven' is often heard, its best iterations offer a robust alternative to the discourse of evidence-based practice, valuing complexity over simplicity, diversity over standardisation and collegiality over individualism. These are, however, not without their challenges. In schools where the intensification of teachers' work is ever increasing, and where teachers are first and foremost sympathetic to their colleagues' classroom and practice difficulties, problems experienced by teachers are immediately 'normalised' (Horn and Little, 2010). Consequently change is often overlooked and ignored because difficulties are 'typical' and 'commonplace' in the lives of all teachers (Casey, 2013).

Conclusions and insights gained

We are not so bold as to presume that the experience of practitioner action research in schools, either our own experiences or the collective experience of school-based teachers-as-researchers, holds the key to success for our colleagues working in early childhood. These (in)sights are offered in the spirit of friendly advice for early childhood educators and academics embarking on practitioner action research, drawn from our work within the 40-year-old tradition we have described above. They are not intended to be exhaustive nor indeed to point towards 'what works' in practitioner inquiry: to do so would be to undermine the argument we have

(Continued)

(Continued)

tried to make, that good practitioner inquiry pushes back on the 'what works/best practice' agenda to understand education as contextual and nuanced. These principles have emerged from our joint experience and reflection as 'insider' and 'outsider' practitioner researchers.

Good practitioner research starts with (and continues to focus on) the concerns, problems and issues of practitioners

This lesson may seem obvious, but the history of action research in schools is strewn with examples of action research 'projects' imposed upon teachers, complete with pre-derived research questions and methods. Good practitioner research emerges from the shared concerns and questions of practitioners about their practice, and is temporally and spatially situated.

Good practitioner research is a collective effort

While the research on practitioner research is increasingly enriched by examples of individual practitioners who engage in classroom or practice-based inquiry (see Ashley's work), we would suggest that there are possibly many more examples of such projects that have been unable to overcome the isolation that can come from such an undertaking. While we acknowledge (from personal experience) such work to be personally and professionally rewarding, the most powerful practitioner action research builds authentic collegiality and integrates a range of different perspectives. From the 'making sense' of data to the integration of different voices, the shared professional discourse and decision-making, one of the great benefits of practitioner inquiry is the capacity of the process to build community and shared understanding of practice.

Good practitioner research takes a 'forensic' rather than 'adversarial' approach to evidence

Searching for incontrovertible truths about 'what works' is, as we have argued above, a highly problematic endeavour. A 'forensic' (Groundwater-Smith and Mockler, 2009) approach to evidence seeks to shed light on a phenomenon, to draw on the wisdom of the research team to develop an understanding of the evidence, and to draw out and appreciate the always various shades of grey.

Good practitioner research welcomes the unwelcome

While the celebration of good practice is often a welcome outcome from practitioner research, a more generative outcome with greater potential impact (both individually and within the community) is that which turns a critical eye on practice and is open to the 'unwelcome truths' that may be uncovered. Of course, the level of openness to the unwelcome often depends upon the level of genuine collegiality and trust established within the research team (or indeed with oneself), but pushing 'beyond celebration' is a worthy goal for beginning practitioner action researchers.

Good practitioner research is ethical practice

From the macro dimensions to the micro practices in which teachers engage when they conduct research, good practitioner research is steeped in an appreciation of ethical practice and a desire to 'do no harm'. Accordingly, good practitioner research is carefully planned and executed, drawing on principles of both research ethics and professional ethics.

We have observed that practitioner action research holds strong transformative power: capacity to transform individuals, communities and the structures that both enable and inhibit student learning and 'success' at school. Our experience indicates that Dadds (1998: 5–6) was correct in her assessment of the potential of practitioner inquiry:

> At the heart of every practitioner research project there is a significant job of work to be done that will make a small contribution to the improvement of the human condition in that context. Good practitioner research ... helps to develop life for others in caring, equitable, humanising ways.

Ongoing research considerations

- How do our recounted experiences of practitioner research in schools resonate with yours in early childhood settings? What are the key differences?
- How do you respond to the principles presented in the conclusion of this chapter? How might you work to incorporate these into your own practitioner research endeavours?

References

Atkinson, E. (2000) 'In defence of ideas, or why "what works" is not enough', *British Journal of Sociology of Education*, 21 (3): 307–30.

Australian Institute for Teaching and School Leadership (2012a) AITSL Website – Certification Evidence. Retrieved from: www.teacherstandards.aitsl.edu.au/certificationevidence (30 January 2013).

Australian Institute for Teaching and School Leadership (2012b) *Australian Teacher Performance and Development Framework*. Melbourne: Australian Institute for Teaching and School Leadership.

Berthoff, A. (1987) 'The teacher as researcher', in D. Goswami and P. R. Stillman (eds), *Reclaiming the Classroom: Teacher Research as an Agency for Change*. New Jersey: Boynton/Cook, pp. 75–86.

Biesta, G. (2014) 'Evidence based practice in education: between science and democracy', in A. Reid, E. P. Hart and M. Peters (eds), *A Companion to Research in Education*. Dordrecht: Springer, pp. 391–400.

Carr, W. (1980) 'The gap between theory and practice', *Journal of Further and Higher Education*, 4: 60–9.

Carr, W. and Kemmis, S. (1986) *Becoming Critical: Education, Knowledge and Action Research*. London: Falmer Press.

Casey, A. (2013) '"Seeing the trees not just the wood": steps and not just journeys in teacher action research', *Educational Action Research*, 21 (2): 147–63.

Casey, A., Dyson, B. and Campbell, A. (2009) 'Action research in physical education: Focusing beyond myself through cooperative learning', *Educational Action Research*, 17 (3): 407–23.

Casey, A. and Goodyear, V.A. (2015) 'Can Cooperative Learning achieve the four learning outcomes of physical education?: A Review of Literature', *QUEST*, 67(1), 56-72. doi: 10.1080/00336297.2014.984733.

Cochran-Smith, M. and Lytle, S. (1999) 'The Teacher Research Movement: a decade later', *Educational Researcher*, 28 (7): 15–25.

Cochran-Smith, M. and Lytle, S. L. (2007) 'Everything's ethics', in A. Campbell and S. Groundwater-Smith (eds), *An Ethical Approach to Practitioner Research: Dealing with Issues and Dilemmas in Action Research*. London: Routledge, pp. 24–41.

Corey, S. (1949) 'Action research, fundamental research, and educational practices', *The Teachers College Record*, 50 (8): 509–14.

Cuttance, P. (2001) *School Innovation: Pathway to the Knowledge Society*. Canberra: Commonwealth of Australia/Department of Education, Training and Youth Affairs.

Dadds, M. (1998) 'Supporting practitioner research: a challenge', *Educational Action Research*, 6 (1): 39–52.

Department of Education Employment and Workplace Relations (2009) *Belonging, Being & Becoming: The Early Years Learning Framework for Australia*. Barton, ACT: Council of Australian Governments/Commonwealth of Australia.

Eisenhart, M. and Towne, L. (2003) 'Contestation and change in national policy on "scientifically based" education research', *Educational Researcher*, 32 (7): 31–8.

Elementary and Secondary Education Act (USA) (2001),   Pub. L. No. 107–110, 115 Stat. 1425

Elliott, J. (1991) *Action Research for Educational Change*. Open University Press: Milton Keynes. Available at: https://professorjohnelliott.wordpress.com/publi cations/ (last accessed 10 June 2015).

Elliott, J. (1997) 'School-based curriculum development and action research', in S. Hollingsworth (ed.), *International Action Research: A Casebook for Educational Reform*. London: Falmer, pp. 17–29.

Elliott, J. (2001) 'Making evidence-based practice educational', *British Educational Research Journal*, 27 (5): 555–74.

Elliott, J. (2007) *Reflecting Where the Action Is: The Selected Writings of John Elliott, World Library of Educationalists*. Routledge: London and New York.

Feldman, A. (1996) 'Enhancing the practice of physics teachers: mechanisms for the generation and sharing of knowledge and understanding in collaborative action research', *Journal of Research in Science Teaching*, 33 (5): 513–40.

Goldacre, B. (2013) *Building Evidence into Education*. London: Department for Education.

Goswami, D. and Stillman, P. R. (eds) (1987) *Reclaiming the Classroom: Teacher Research as an Agency for Change*. New Jersey: Boynton/Cook.

Groundwater-Smith, S. (1998) 'Putting teacher professional judgement to work', *Educational Action Research*, 6 (1): 21–37.

Groundwater-Smith, S. and Mockler, N. (2009) *Teacher Professional Learning in an Age of Compliance: Mind the Gap*. Dordrecht: Springer.

Grundy, S. (1994) 'Action research at the school level: possibilities and problems', *Educational Action Research*, 2 (1): 23–37.

Grundy, S. (1995) *Action Research as Professional Development*. Murdoch, WA: Innovative Links Project.

Habermas, J. (1987) *Theory of Communicative Action, Volume 2: System and Lifeworld: The Critique of Functionalist Reason*, trans. T. McCarthy. Boston: Beacon.

Hammersley, M. (1997) 'Educational research and teaching: a response to David Hargreaves' TTA Lecture', *British Educational Research Journal*, 23: 141–61.

Hargreaves, D. (2007) 'Teaching as a research based profession: possibilities and prospects' (Teacher Training Agency Lecture, 1996), in M. Hammersley (ed.), *Educational Research and Evidence-based Practice*. Milton Keynes/London: Open University Press/Sage, pp. 3–18.

Horn, I. S. and Little, J. W. (2010) 'Attending to problems of practice: routines and resources for professional learning in teachers' workplace interactions', *American Educational Research Journal*, 47 (1): 181–217.

Kemmis, S. (2006) 'Participatory action research and the public sphere', *Educational Action Research*, 14 (4): 459–76.

Kemmis, S. (2011) 'A self-reflective practitioner and a new definition of critical participatory action research', in N. Mockler and J. Sachs (eds), *Rethinking Educational Practice through Reflexive Inquiry*. Dordrecht: Springer, pp. 11–29.

Kemmis, S. and Grundy, S. (1997) 'Educational action research in Australia: organisations and practice', in S. Hollingsworth (ed.), *International Action Research: A Casebook for Educational Reform*. London: Falmer: 40-48.

Kirk, D. (2011) *Physical Education: Major Themes in Education*. Abingdon: Routledge.

Lather, P. (2010) *Engaging Science Policy: From the Side of the Messy*. New York: Peter Lang.

Lewin, K. (1946) *Resolving Social Conflicts*. New York: Harper and Row.

Mockler, N. (2013) 'The slippery slope to efficiency? An Australian perspective on school/university partnerships for teacher professional learning', *Cambridge Journal of Education*, 42 (3): 273–89.

Mockler, N. and Groundwater-Smith, S. (2015a) *Student Voice: Beyond Legitimation and Guardianship*. Dordrecht: Springer.

Mockler, N. and Groundwater-Smith, S. (2015b) 'Seeking for the unwelcome truths: beyond celebration in inquiry-based teacher professional learning', *Teachers and Teaching: Theory and Practice*, 22 (1).

Noffke, S. (1994) 'Action research: towards the next generation', *Educational Action Research*, 2 (1): 9–12.

Noffke, S. (1997) 'Themes and tensions in US action research: towards historical analysis', in S. Hollingsworth (ed.), *International Action Research: A Casebook for Educational Reform*. London: Falmer, pp. 2–16.

Noffke, S. and Zeichner, K. (1987) 'Action research and teacher thinking: the first phase of the action research on Action Research Project at the University of Wisconsin – Madison', paper presented at the American Educational Research Association Annual Meeting, Washington, DC.

Sachs, J. (1999) 'Using teacher research as a basis for professional renewal', *Journal of Inservice Education*, 25 (1): 39–53.

Slavin, R. (2002) 'Evidence-based education policies: transforming educational practice and research', *Educational Researcher*, 31 (7): 15–21.

Stenhouse, L. (1983) 'Research as a basis for teaching', in L. Stenhouse (ed.), *Authority, Education and Emancipation*. London: Heinemann: 177–195.

Tinning, R. I. (1991) 'Teacher education pedagogy: dominant discourses and the process of problem setting', *Journal of Teaching in Physical Education*, 11: 1–20.

Tinning, R. (2012) 'A socially critical HPE (aka physical education) and the challenge for teacher education', in B. Down and J. Smyth (eds), *Critical Voices in Teacher Education*. Dordrecht: Springer, pp. 223–38.

Zeichner, K. (2001) 'Educational action research', in H. Bradbury and P. Reason (eds), *Handbook of Action Research*. Newbury Park: Sage, pp. 273–84.

Zeichner, K. M. (2003) 'Teacher research as professional development for P-12 educators in the USA', *Educational Action Research*, 11 (2): 301–26.

Zeichner, K. and Noffke, S. (2001) 'Practitioner research', in V. Richardson (ed.), *Handbook of Research on Teaching*. Washington, DC: AERA, pp. 298–330.

INDEX

WITHDRAWN